THE SELECTION OF A SACRED STRAWBERRY

WINNING STORIES FROM PENFLUENZA III

WRITEFLUENCE

Copyright © Writefluence
All Rights Reserved.

This book has been self-published with all reasonable efforts taken to make the material error-free by the author. No part of this book shall be used, reproduced in any manner whatsoever without written permission from the author, except in the case of brief quotations embodied in critical articles and reviews.

The Author of this book is solely responsible and liable for its content including but not limited to the views, representations, descriptions, statements, information, opinions and references ["Content"]. The Content of this book shall not constitute or be construed or deemed to reflect the opinion or expression of the Publisher or Editor. Neither the Publisher nor Editor endorse or approve the Content of this book or guarantee the reliability, accuracy or completeness of the Content published herein and do not make any representations or warranties of any kind, express or implied, including but not limited to the implied warranties of merchantability, fitness for a particular purpose. The Publisher and Editor shall not be liable whatsoever for any errors, omissions, whether such errors or omissions result from negligence, accident, or any other cause or claims for loss or damages of any kind, including without limitation, indirect or consequential loss or damage arising out of use, inability to use, or about the reliability, accuracy or sufficiency of the information contained in this book.

Made with ♥ on the Notion Press Platform
www.notionpress.com

To writers everywhere...

Contents

Acknowledgements	vii
About The Authors In This Book	ix
About Our Jury	xix
1. Blackbird, Blackbird	1
2. The Resolution	12
3. Sacrament 1.05 - The Unsexy Occult	25
4. The Shiroyama Ritual	37
5. The Longest Night In The Darkest Forest	48
6. The Magic Chimney	58
7. Mr. Johnson's Formulas	68
8. An Uprooted Presence	77
9. True Love	87
10. The Ritual	96
11. Out Of The Fire	104
12. Treading On Eggshells	113
13. The Selection Of A Sacred Strawberry	122
14. The Red Fishing Boat	131
15. Kavya	139
16. The Art Of Tapping Into Fame	147
17. Unearthed	157
18. Nityasumangali	166
19. To Simran	174
20. The Trials Of Marcus	183
21. Perfect Plot	191

Contents

22. The Ritual Of The Red Moon		198
23. The Peepal Tree Temple		205
24. My Confession		213
25. The Midnight Ritual		220
26. The Lighthouse Keeper		228
27. The Sacrifice Bearer		236
28. Blue Dendrobium		243
Books By Writefluence		253

Acknowledgements

Team WriteFluence would like to thank our jury members who have been consistently helping us for over two years in selecting the best stories for our compilations. Also, a huge thank you to all the participants and winning writers for making PenFluenza a successful yearly event!

About The Authors In This Book

1. Aboli Mane currently blogs short stories and poetry on her blog A Writer In The Room. A published poet, she published her debut poetry book "An Aster's Solitude" in 2019. Her poems were included in anthologies like Foraging by Globalage Poetry and Secrets by the Write Order. She switched to writing short stories due to her deep love of creating new characters and worlds. Her stories often have a fantastical or folkloric twist. A Mumbaikar, she currently resides in Goa. You can reach her on Instagram at @aboli_poetry.
2. Adyasha is currently studying as a final year MBBS student in Bhubaneswar. She is a voracious reader and her preferred genres are fantasy and science-fiction. In her pastime, she likes to pen down stories. She has published two novels previously- "The Fearless Warriors" (2015) and "The Guardian (2021)" and a short sorry titled "Nexus" in the Indian Periodical Magazine (October 2022).
3. Aneesha Shewani (she/her) works as a full-time technical writer and editor in India. She is an avid reader and frequently blogs at www.bluepenstrokes.com. Her poetry and short stories are published in various anthologies. She is also a book reviewer for Reedsy Discovery. She loves to watch Netflix and also spends time learning about emerging technologies and trends in content creation.
4. Anoushka Boodhna, 41, is a child of Mauritian immigrants to the UK. Over the last few years, her writing has explored storytelling on death, loss, grief,

love, and belonging, combining different genres, namely, science fiction, fantasy, ghost story, and mystery, and drawing from Hindu and Buddhist spirituality. She enjoys thinking about how the world is complex and how it could be and should be different. She wants to write stories for women in their forties, Women who are at a crossroads; who are rich with experience, knowledge, and wisdom, and confronting the different types of harm done to them over time and now seeking answers and truths to move forward into the next life stage.

5. Arria Haigler is a first-year college student who is hoping to get a degree in English to follow her dream—of being a full-time author. Her favorite genres are fiction, fantasy, and pretty much all things mystical and made-up, and she's hoping she can get a laugh out of her reader in almost everything she writes. Her crowning achievement was making it into an anthology with a short story called "Evergreen" in high school and she's currently trying to make it out of her one-hit wonder phase. Purple has been her color for as long as she can remember, and it probably will be for many years to come.

6. Bethany Taylor is a UK-based writer who has always had a passion for literature and writing since an early age. Currently a Creative Writing student, she has crafted fictional tales of various genres, ranging from the cheesiest romance to the eeriest horror. In her spare time, she enjoys reading modern classics, especially books by writers like Terry Pratchett and Khaled Hosseini. Her favorite book of all time is The Kite Runner, which she reviews as "the most heart-wrenching, soul-destroying book that everyone should

ABOUT THE AUTHORS IN THIS BOOK

read". She also enjoys going to the theatre, as well as purchasing books for friends and family which collect dust on shelves.

7. Bhavna Jagnani is a third-year student from India. She loves to read and write and aspires to become a writer. Her story 'The Holy Grail' has won in the LGBTO Romance/ Betrayal short story contest organized by WriteFluence in July-August 2021 and has been published in the book A Lie On Her Lips. Her story 'Hidden, Can You See It?' has won the short story contest PenFuenza 2.0 organized by WriteFluence in December 2021-January 2022 and has been published in the book Sepia.

8. Denarii Peters was born in the northwest of England. She now lives with her husband in the county of Norfolk, where the weather is much drier. She is often to be found reading or spying on a small herd of muntjac deer that have taken up residence in the gardens outside her ground-floor flat. A former primary school teacher, she now spends her days writing stories of all kinds and drinking a lot of coffee. She is currently working on a collection of linked ghost stories as well as putting the finishing touches to a series of young adult fantasy novels. In the last year eight of her other short stories have been or are soon to be published in various anthologies, including two with WriteFluence.

9. Emecheta Christian is an author known for his unique style of storytelling. His writing is heavily influenced by his experiences growing up in Nigeria, and it's characterized by a deep understanding of Nigerian culture and society. He is particularly skilled at weaving conflict and wit into his work, making it both entertaining and thought-provoking. His works have

earned critical acclaim and have been widely praised for their ability to tackle important social issues in a relatable and accessible way. We strongly believe that Emecheta Christian is going to become a respected figure in the literary world someday.

10. Gayathri Sampath navigates the world of corporate strategy by day, armed with her education and experience, and by night transforms into a dreamer who inhabits a fantastical wonderland, drawing sustenance from her imagination and love for writing. She wears many hats management consultant, academician, leadership coach, creative thinker, and writer. She raises two handsome and charming young men (in her fond eyes!) with her amicable and long-suffering spouse in Mumbai. She is a lifelong reader and can eat fantasy for breakfast, thrillers for lunch, and romance for dinner. Alas, her job as a Professor of Strategy at a fast-growing private university, demands she also read and write the occasional research paper! She has published her short stories as part of two anthologies and an e-novella on Amazon. She is currently working on a full-length fantasy novel for young adults, set in ancient India and Korea. The novel draws upon folklore, myth, fact, and history to craft a compelling story

11. Gitanjali Maria is a market analyst and content writer. Her short stories have been published in various anthologies and websites such as eFiction India, Stories of the Nature of Cities, and IndusWomanWriting. She has also published a collection of short stories on environmental issues titled 'A Wake Up Call'. She is an advocate of the slogan "reuse and recycle." Creating junk art is another of her favorite hobbies.

12. Based on Australia's Gold Coast, Jay is a writer,

performing arts teacher, qualified clinical hypnotherapist, and mum. She has lived in the UK, Greece, Indonesia, Australia, and Singapore. Her short stories, flash, and micros have been published online at Cafe Lit Magazine, Reedsy, Globe Soup, Vocal, Sadie Tells Stories, Save As, and Off Topic. In print, Jay's work has been published in Mr. Rosewood, Fabula Nivalis, Leicester Writes, The Gift, and Crimson, and will be featured in Unleash Lit Magazine and Cerasus Magazine in early 2023. She has received numerous awards, long and shortlist for her fiction. She is a two-time winner of The Australian Writers Centre's Furious Fiction and winner of the 2022 Exeter Story Prize. Her debut novel will be published in 2023 with Australian indie press Serenade Publishing.

13. Kitiera Morey is a lively perfectionist with the mouth of a drunken sailor. When she's not singing off-key for the entire world to hear or chasing after the chaos demon masquerading as her toddler, Kitiera searches for the next action-adventure or supernatural book to devour in a single night. She lives in New York with her boyfriend and horde of furry companions and is currently working on too many stories to count.

14. An ex-English teacher with a passion for exploring the macabre, other-worldly, and darkness, Lee Fountain is a short story writer, currently working on his first novel with the working title Wish Wolf.

15. Lisa Cortez has been telling stories since she was a child growing up in London and was only allowed to play outside on a concrete driveway. She would invite the neighborhood kids over and lead them in all kinds of imaginative games. Her imagination took over and has never surrendered its hold on her. She enjoys writing

short stories with a twist based on events she's experienced or heard about. In 2022, she won first prize in both the Short Story Unlimited Summer competition and the Northern Beaches Writers Competition. Her unpublished novel The Proveniste was one of twenty longlisted entries out of 700 in the Richell Prize of 2022.

16. Michael Noonan lives in Halifax (famous for its Piece Hall), West Yorkshire, and has had stories and articles published in anthologies and artworks accepted by literary magazines, in the UK, Europe, and the US. A volume of his short stories, entitled, Seven Tall Tales, is available at Amazon, as a book or on Kindle. His comic one-act play, entitled, Elvis and the Psychiatrist, has been shown at the Snowdance ten-minute comedy festival at the Sixth Theatre in Racine Wisconsin, and a one-act play of his, The Restive Audience, has been published in the anthology volume, Hello Godot by Freshwords International literary magazine.

17. Ninad Bhangle is a business strategy professional by day and a writer by night. Born and brought up in Mumbai but now settled in Bangalore, he has completed his engineering from VJTI, Mumbai, and his MBA from IIM-Indore. Writing has always been his passion since his school days when he penned four short stories named "The Clever Andrews", hugely inspired by Enid Blyton's books. During his college days, he dabbled into writing poetry and thrillers which continue to be a passion even now. He has published two poetry books, "Unspoken - Musings on Love, Loss and Life" and "Unbroken - Musings on Dreams, Hope and Life". He is also a published TinyTale author through "Terribly Tiny Tales" and "The Scribbled Stories" platforms. When he is not writing or working, Ninad enjoys reading,

traveling, and loves exploring new cultures and cuisines.
18. Oluwatoyin Magbagbeola is a writer from Nigeria. She found an online magazine called Afrovibe magazine that writes about Africa's history, culture, food, and lifestyle. She's also a tech enthusiast.
19. Peter Collins is a writer specializing in short stories. He has had over a dozen stories published in hard-copy anthologies and many more published online. His writing often features a quirky sense of humor and an unexpected twist. He has won a number of prizes for his writing and in 2021 was awarded the HG Wells Fiction Prize. He lives in Leeds, England, and when not writing is often out in the Yorkshire countryside either cycling or walking his dog, Saski.
20. Philip Stenström (born 1987) is a short story writer from Gotland. He has published various short stories in many anthologies. His writing is usually characterized by nature, city, and countryside in light of his upbringing on a farm on the island of Gotland in the Baltic Sea.
21. Priya Nayak-Gole is a pediatric Speech-Language Pathologist by profession and a writer by passion. She loved to dabble in thrillers and erotica most of the time. She self-published her first book in 2020 August and the second manuscript is currently awaiting a publisher. She had written nine episodic novels on social platforms and all of them can be read on her website www.fictionvilla.com. She also participates on select platforms for writing flash fiction across genres. Her articles have been published on popular sites like women's web. She recently won the jury's choice for the most impactful contribution in 2022 on a popular website. She intends to spread awareness of disability

awareness, social evils, and mental health through her writeups.

22. Prosper Ugbosu-Joe is a writer and creative artist with a passion for storytelling. He has always been drawn to the supernatural and the mysteries of the universe, and this can be seen in his writing. When he's not writing, Prosper can be found tinkering with his latest art project or lost in a good book. He believes that the power of storytelling can bring people together and inspire change in the world.

23. Ramya V. is an IT professional who delves into the world of books. A voracious reader who believes the pen is mightier to bring about a change. She dedicates her time to writing stories and poems in English and Tamil. She picks her pen to write when she stumbles upon any social incident that she feels needs attention. Writing fiction inspired by real-life incidents tops her list. In 2018, she also won the event – 'Which quote of Mahatma Gandhi changed your heart' hosted by the Gandhi World Foundation. She has contributed and won as a co-author to more than forty anthologies in prose and poetry. Her works are regularly published on online sites such as Women's Web and Women's Web Tamil. She is also a recipient of Literoma Author Achiever Award 2021. Her stories bagged a place in the top ten list of the 'Annual Micro Fiction 2021' contest hosted by Half Baked Beans under the categories 'Horror' and 'Erotica'. She received a certification of appreciation for her poem in the Annual Wordsmith Award 2021 hosted by the Asian Literary Society. She is also the editor of the poetry anthologies "Anklets in my Hands", "When Fire spoke to Water" and the anthology 'The Femme of Animal Kingdom'. She also received multiple awards for

her debut book published in 2021. She was shortlisted for the Orange Flower Awards 2022 hosted by Women's Web. In 2022, she received a certificate of excellence awarded for "Indian Women Rising Star" under the category 'Literature' from the Asian Literary Society. She won third place for English Poetry in ALS WORDSMITH AWARD 2022 and received a certificate of excellence for English Story and Writing on women's issues from the Asian Literary Society in 2022.

24. Samantha Pinazza is an Italian lawyer. She grew up in the beautiful Dolomites and her dream is to become a writer. In March, in Italy, they will publish her first novel "Caliburn", but for her, this is only the beginning. Samantha loves to travel, discover new places, and live wonderful adventures. In her free time, she used to read and practice kickboxing.

25. Sohini Roy is a twenty-one years old artist, based in Kolkata, West Bengal, India. Born into a small, middle-class, Bengali family, she graduated from South Point High School in 2019. Roy is currently pursuing an undergraduate course in the Department of Chemistry, at Calcutta University. But her mind has always led her into digging deep inside her conscience. It's always asked what that small child residing in her wants to do to make a silent, but noticeable change in the predictable patterns of the modern world. That's what drives her to join those small experiences she has here and there, and add some meaning to them with her own emotions. Roy now aspires to become a successful '*illustrauthor*'. Something that would hold both her art and her words. She wishes to work in the fields of comics and graphic novels, to give the audience a better and more enriched experience through the pages of a book. It's her dream

to see people choosing the brown pages of an old book rather than the over-brightened screens of fancy gadgets.

26. Vaibhav Pradeep Gilankar has been writing stories in fantasy and macabre genres for the past 7+ years. He's been running his blog "Through the Eyes of a Writer by Vaibhav Gilankar" on which he has published his fantasy and children's stories. A children's poetry anthology called "Written With The Rays of Rhyme" has also been self-published by him on Amazon. On Medium and Wattpad he frequently posts his poems and macabre tales. He likes to consider himself a "Storysmith", engaging and surprising his readers through his tales has always been his favorite hobby. To achieve the highest recognition in the realm of literature is his dream.

27. Will is a writer from Sweden with an interest in dark history, the supernatural, and psychology. He lives together with the ragdoll kitten named Loke - a name that is very fitting for his mischievous personality. Growing up in the countryside, Will spent most of his time reading books and dreaming up his own fantasy worlds and characters, and as his interest in storytelling grew he decided to study media production and then went on to study screenwriting.

28. Inspired by the writings of L. Frank Baum as a child and Edgar Rice Burroughs as an adult, Andrew K. Edgars aspires to create worlds that will capture the imagination and entertain the mind. A resident of North Texas, home has always been the Land of OZ, amongst the Thark of Barsoom, or with The Doctor in The TARDIS.

About Our Jury

Vipul Shaalmali Raut is an illustrious educationist with over 17 years of experience in teaching, mentoring, and leadership roles. He loves reading George Eliot and has read The Mill on the Floss more than 5 times. He loves to read and re-read old classics and states that each time he finishes a book perceiving the story differently.

In recent years, Raut has been engaged in conducting various workshops on creative writing and career development. When he's not reading, he is either watching movies or theatrical plays.

Raut's WriteFluencing Mantra is: "A poor reader cannot become a good writer."

Amanda Schmidt has been teaching English throughout her 23+ years of career at various renowned institutions in four different nations at different times. She has also worked as an instructional designer, written procedures, and designed courses for new-recruit professors with her previous employer. For the last 6 years, Schmidt has been an active part of an internal magazine 'Wordy Percussion' with her current employer in Singapore and was appointed as the Editor in 2020 as a recognition of her constant efforts to innovate with the magazine. Schmidt loves reading Gillian Flynn, Ruth Ware, and Dean Koontz. She has been an avid P.G. Wodehouse reader throughout her teens. When she isn't reading, Schmidt loves to watch travel-related documentaries online and make plans for her next travel destination.

Schmidt's WriteFluencing Mantra is: "Read more to write better!"

ABOUT OUR JURY

Palash Basak has been working as a technical writer in a reputed organization in Bengaluru since 2015. He loves reading and writing fiction and vouches that watching old classics by Satyajit Ray, Bimal Roy or Guru Dutt can kill that dreaded writer's block. After having graduated and worked as a clerk for 8 years, Basak decided to complete his Masters in Mass Communication in 2001. Post that, he worked in several firms in the capacity of a Business Communications writer. He believes in the continuous process of learning and evolving and has enrolled himself into learning various creative writing and technical writing courses on self-learning apps. He is a die-hard Gulzar fan. He loves to read old classics in English and Bengali. When he's not reading or writing; he is helping his daughter-in-law cope with the tantrums of his 18-month-old grand-son.

Basak's WriteFluencing Mantra is: "Writing a perfect novel may take years and a perfect writer may always want to go back and keep making changes to that very perfect novel every year!"

Kaumudi Amrute's writing workshops have received several amazing reviews from students of different age groups. Amrute is a retired educationist and has spread her wings now with the initiative of her small cultural venture 'Kalaa Kalpana' where she conducts short-term writing workshops for all age groups and also runs handicraft workshops with the help of her students.

When she's not teaching, Amrute loves to knit, bake and conduct experiments in the kitchen. Amrute lives in Wilmington with her husband and a dog; and loves reading Christina Rossetti, Sylvia Plath, and Phillis Wheatley.

Amrute's WriteFluencing Mantra is: "A good story is what a writer writes and re-writes several times until it is ready to reach impeccability in the eyes of a reader."

ABOUT OUR JURY

Arvind Solanki has been writing content for various websites, brands, and products since 1998 and has also worked on a few projects as a ghostwriter. His expertise lies in writing and editing children's books and blogs. He has worked on more than 20 websites to create content for children related to general knowledge and stories. When Arvind isn't working on his writing projects, he loves to travel, watch sports, play with his four-year-old son, and lose arguments with his wife.

Arvind's WriteFluencing Mantra is: "A good writer will first read! Especially, a contest's guidelines."

The ritual of life, so sweet
A timeless tradition shared.
A thing of beauty, a blessing in disguise,
A reminder of strength, a way to open our eyes.
An answer found in silence,
a peace that's deep and wise,
A gateway to the soul's true essence,
a way to reach the skies.
A fire burns bright, smoke begins to swirl,
As the embers of love start to unfurl.
Drums beat rhythmically, like a sacred heart,
The music of transformation becomes a work of art.
The sacred chants of ancestors fill the air,
As a transformation begins to take shape and care.
A sacred energy binds together,
with a love that is pure and true,
The energies of the elements
that make everything alright.
And in the heart of the ritual,
the beauty of transformation is seen,
As the fire of passion and transformation
burns bright and clean.

Sneha Acharekar

CHAPTER ONE

Blackbird, Blackbird

By Arria Haigler

There was a tune I liked to whistle when I was riding home through the forest. Past the meandering rivulet that ran an icy blue, under the trees that swung weightlessly and dropped leaves like swirling, dancing sprites.

"What's it called, Chroma? The name of this song mom taught me to whistle?" I combed her jet black mane with my fingers as I asked her.

She let out some gum-flapping sound.

"Yeah, I don't remember either."

Chroma and I kept trotting along to the song, like we did almost every day, haunted by the nameless tune that flowed forth from my lips and followed us like the ghost of the woman who'd taught it to me.

"I like it much better than her other song. That song."

Chroma stopped dead in her tracks, and turned her head slightly to the left, peering somewhere deep into the forest across the rivulet.

As we silently gazed at a separation between the trees on the other side of the rivulet, a flock of birds frenzied into the sky from the deep forest in that direction.

"One, two, three...yellow, yellow, red...damn. Seven birds and not one of them darker than the bark on these oak trees."

Chroma forced some air through her nose, still focused on the forest.

"I know, I know. It's the wrong thing to wish for. You're no fun, CC. I just want to see what would happen if someone really saw one. Nothing good, no doubt, but...it would be something."

I pulled Chroma's reins in the direction she was looking and gave her a soft jab with my heel. She did not flinch.

"C'mon, Chroma, you don't want to go see what spooked those birds?"

The rivulet babbled over Chroma's silence.

"It'll be quick, Chroma! I bet there's a whole flock of ripe, orange carrots that scared all those birds over there! Or applesss!"

She shook her head swiftly before stepping decidedly into the shallow water. She walked between the separation of the trees and entered the thick brush beyond the separation.

As we drew deeper into the forest, the ground grew more uneven, and trees harder to slip past until we reached a downward incline, and Chroma refused to transport me any longer.

I dismounted and scratched her velvety black chin, "I'll be back really quick. I think there's a clearing between those trees on the other side of this incline, I'm sure that's where the birds came from."

She had nothing to offer me but a hoarse whine.

I slipped down the incline and shoved through the shrubbery that separated me from the clearing. In the center sat someone very familiar with a horribly foreign look of despair captivating his entire person.

"Hey, Corrine, who killed your pup...py..."

Corrine was sitting in the center of the clearing in front of a bolder, hands, always littered with bronze rings, clasped so tightly his knuckles were white and a tear approached the tip of his chin. I shifted my eyes to what he was conducting his morose prayer at.

On the boulder, there the cursed thing sat.

A blackbird.

"You—you found a blackbird...Corrine, you're the first person to ever see a blackbird!"

"Hush."

"Hush? Corrine, please, I could beat you up with an empty pillow cas—"

He whipped around to face me. "Hush! Are you too arrogant to see what's right in front of you?! You of all people should be horrified! You are the Health-Keeper's daughter! And some of us believe in the tried and true traditions keeping the health of this land, no matter what highbrow 'science' you claim!"

I clenched my fist, "'May she rest in peace'."

"What?"

"You forgot 'May she rest in peace'. At least, I figured you forgot, because I didn't need 'science' to tell me that my mom—your precious Health-Keeper—was my only family, and she did only die three weeks ago. Three weeks and three days, to be exact. Since you obviously care so deeply about tradition and respect, I figured you must have forgotten the 'May she rest in peace'."

He turned back to me slightly and took a deep breath. "I'm sorry, Archie. I had no right."

"And don't forget it. Man, I thought being the only young lady in my house would earn me some respect, but pious pricks like yourself keep forgetting," I threw the back of my hand on my forehead, "I'm just a dainty, respectable young woman who just hates to argue!"

Corrine had gone back to whimpering his hymn at the small, orange-beaked bird, which turned its head and watched us both.

"Corrine, praying at the bird won't make you unsee it. If you're really into tradition, then we have to go tell Village Master—"

"Do you believe in luck, Archie?"

I sighed. "This question again." I interlocked my fingers and spoke in a deep, booming voice like the Village Master's. "'There is no luck, only duty. And if we all do our duty to each other, then we won't ever need luck.'"

"I used to believe that. I really did." Another tear formed in his eye and he turned to me. "But a man who sees over fifty blackbirds in a village where there should be none must be unlucky."

"...Over fifty..."

The blackbird began to crow loudly as Corrine sobbed, and I realized the three of us were surrounded by beady black eyes just outside the clearing, watching us, crowing. Frantic wings began to accompany the crowing, and suddenly, a flock of blackbirds was upon us, circling us in the clearing and drawing closer with their demented crowing. Corrine sang his song louder, my mother's song, the song meant to keep them away as they descended on us.

The father and my children

Come gather round my song.

For if the night should take us,
We'll reap eternal dawn.
The evil of the dark shall pass
Come now, it won't be long.
Have faith that your deliverance
Was sown by sinner's foll—y!
Blackbird, blackbird, dark as dusk
Die and you'll deliver us!

But the birds kept closing in.

"Corrine! Let's go! Chroma–!"

He kept singing.

I grabbed his hands and pulled them apart, but he pulled it back, and I was left with one of his bronze rings.

He clasped his hands again. "I am lost."

The blackbirds flocked him, and I bolted for Chroma. Chroma galloped back into the village, and as soon as I dismounted her on the outskirts, I knew that the time had come for me to go. Mom had always told me that I would know when the time was to leave the village, and the first blackbird sighting was all I needed.

Now, all I had to do was head to the shop to get food for the journey.

"Let's hope Hammond's spies aren't on the lookout for me in the middle of the village," I told Chroma as I left her.

As I tried to get to the shop unnoticed, I was so focused on looking over my shoulder that the encounter I feared found its way in front of me.

"Well wishes! Archie! It is good to see you!"

"Ah! I mean, hi. Hello to you as well, Village Master Hammond."

"Yes, it's especially good to see you back so early from your, well, mystical engagements in the forest, but I'm sure one day you'll regale the village with a run-down of your doings out there."

Hammond's loyal groupies listening in on our conversation were nodding in agreement with him.

"Sure. But, right now, I'm going to the shop."

"Oh, yes, the shop! Well, don't forget to pick up some of that tea your mother loved. Really helped soothe her throat after the Herald Cry. It really takes a toll on you, as you know, the cry lasts from sunrise to sunset, and there's no quitting at noon. The Health-Keeper is a vital role in this village, and the month is drawing to a close. We need a new Health-Keeper and I've and I know you won't disappoint, Archie, just like Amara didn't."

I clenched my fist. "Don't pretend to know her."

"Now, Archie, we both admired her very much. And you must understand by now how important it was to her that we watch over each other. It's the duty we owe to each other, after all. If we don't, we fall into chaos. Unimaginable tragedies, all because we can no longer trust each other. Right, Archie?"

My nails pressed so hard into my palms, I thought I may start to bleed. "Agree to disagree, Hammond."

"Well, maybe we can agree to be cautious in those woods. We wouldn't want you to stumble upon those berries that somehow made it into your mother's tea."

I scoffed, "Now you've done it. I was going to let you and your fan club off easy, but if you want chaos, it's yours. Everybody, I saw a blackbird—actually, I saw fifty. Not too far from the village. So it seems we won't be needing a Health-Keeper or a Herald Cry or any of that, because the blackbirds are here, now, and before long, they'll come to shit on all your houses!"

There was a stillness as the village people took in my words. Hammond was staring at me with a glare that could pierce my heart.

Then, screams rose up across the village, followed by the sound of breaking glass. A woman had broken the shop window and held a glass shard to the shopkeeper's throat. A man dropped to his knees and sobbed in the street before someone came and stole from his pockets. Another man could not stop yelling "Blackbird! Blackbird! Blackbird!" Until someone came and punched him in the side of the head. A woman put a knife to her dog's throat.

And endless villagers threw themselves at Hammond, hanging on to his long, gray robes and praying to him, begging him to stop the end of the world coming for them. They were the only thing keeping him away from me as I broke for the shop.

But a woman stood in my path with a knife in hand, calling me the Cursed Child, and I narrowly avoided getting shot with a sharpened arrow whose origin I couldn't tell. The village was on fire, and black towers of smoke engulfed the sky. So with the villagers I'd known since birth clawing at my heels, I ran until I reached Chroma.

And we rode and rode until I couldn't smell smoke anymore.

"If mom was correct, we'll have to ride for a week before we find the next village over...and hopefully she was correct, because she's my only friend left, dead or alive."

Chroma blew air from her nose.

"Let's hope the next village doesn't believe in stupid songs warding off dumb birds."

As we rode, I assessed the things I could sell or barter. I had Corrine's ring and a pouch full of the bright blue berries that had "made their way" into my mom's tea and killed her. When I saw her at the funeral, I had to know what had killed her. It was an image that kept me going back into the forest, looking for some substance that could eat through flesh. Until I finally found bright blue berries I had to hack down into my sack without touching, because they stung my fingertips.

"Can I tell you a secret, Chroma?"

She flapped her gums.

"I don't think mom believed in the Herald Cry. Just like I don't."

But something ripped through the air and interrupted us, sending Chroma into hysteria.

Her front legs flew skyward and she tossed me into the dirt, my head hitting a rock as she sailed through the forest without me, an arrow in her croup.

My eyes began to go crossed, and dizziness mixed with the pain of the collision.

As I drifted off to a foggy sleep, I saw a gray figure approaching me from the forest.

I awoke to see Hammond finish tying my hands and feet together. We were inside one of the back rooms of his chapel. The doors were barred and I could hear distant banging of villagers against the main doors. This small room was filled to the brim with cages of blackbirds.

But like the bird in the clearing, they were sitting quietly, watching.

Hammond walked away and I put my free hand against my pouch on my hip.

"Congratulations. The village is in ruin." He went to a cage and opened it. "They think it's the end—"

"Because that's what you tell us."

Hammond smiled. "Correct, but why?" He took the bird from it's cage, and in a swift movement, without the bird flinching, he chopped its head off.

From the body of the dead bird, a cloud of smoke appeared, and as if we were watching it happen through the blackbird's eyes, a scene played out in the smoke. It was Corrine seeing the blackbird, and deciding what to do.

"I-I could tell Village Master Hammond...but...what if he believes I'm cursed? Surely...that will be the end for me..." He dropped to his knees, clasped his hands, and begged the lord for forgiveness.

Hammond waved the smoke away and threw the dead bird in a bin. "Lovely boy. Devout boy. But this is why I preach the importance of doing our duty for each other. The villagers, they get scared, they take their own way, they're human, how can I blame them? But, that means more work for me. I do things I don't want to do, I make up myths, I tell the villagers they must tell me if they see blackbirds. And most of the time, they do. But if they don't...well, hundreds of birds join my ranks."

"What are you talking about?"

He dug in his pocket and found a ring, a bronze ring.

"What did you do to Corrine?!"

"No, it's what did Corrine do to Corrine. He believed in that song more than he believed in me." He motioned to the cages full of birds with familiar eyes. "This is what happens when I sow the seeds of obedience, honesty, trust between my villagers and I and they refuse to cooperate. A lack of cooperation makes chaos, and you and that mother of your specialize in chaos."

"Don't talk about my—"

"We could've had an empire. All she had to do was sing her song, stand in the chapel and sing, let me worry about the consequences. But she couldn't cope. She couldn't understand why she had to stand out there and ward off blackbirds for the villagers out there when her beautiful voice was creating blackbirds back here. She was always asking 'why'. Order. Order is why. People are good at believing, for the most part, but they stray. And when they do, I test their belief in me, as their leader, as their Master. You see a blackbird, and all you have to do is tell me, the Village Master. But if you don't, the Herald Cry makes you another spy that watches over my village for me. Protects it for me. Simple, if you can live with the guilt. But she just couldn't believe, it wasn't right to test the villagers with a sign of certain death. But let me ask you, what shows better allegiance to your village than admitting it's in certain peril? And that's all you have to do, show me you can look death in the eye and still put your village first. And if not, you end up like poor, sweet Corrine there."

A blackbird captivated with despair sat in a cage next to me over several, tarnished rings.

"You are not the leader of a village. You are the leader of mindless horde that doesn't know its own thoughts from yours. The only real freedom they've ever experienced was when they decided to burn this village to the ground."

Hammond shook his head and laughed. "Archangel."

"Shut up."

"What a ridiculous name for a baby girl. And what's worse, you grew to choose 'Archie' as your nickname."

"Don't talk about her."

"I am not talking about her, I'm talking about you. Such a devout name for such a godless child. A funny name at best, made all the more hilarious by its owner...But your mother? She lost it at the end, but she was a good woman. It's a shame, a real shame how she went out, her face destroyed by the poison, a gaping hole from her chin down her throat where it ate her flesh. Pity she won't be able to sing in the next life."

As he came to stand in front of me, I began to laugh. Then, my laugh grew until I was chuckling uncontrollably.

Hammond sighed. "What is it, child? Tell me your final thoughts as you're about to join your mother."

"It took one day to burn the village down that you spent your life building. And it's only going to take seconds for the poison to eat through your flesh."

I shoved my hand into my pocket and ignored the excruciating pain of the poison berries eating through the palm of my hand and threw them against his face. They bursted in a brilliant and boiling splatter against the side of his face, eating away at him until the white of his skull was almost completely exposed.

I untied the rope on my hands with my teeth and found the key to the bird cages on his belt loop. I unlocked them, a task that took at least an hour, but the birds stayed in their cages. I unbarred the door and shoved it open to the astonishment of several rioting villagers.

I stood looking out at my village in chaos, their dead Master behind me, and the blackbirds finally flew out to rejoin their village.

CHAPTER TWO

The Resolution

By Priya Nayak Gole

Prologue

She dashed through the darkness, the petrichor boscage, joining a gusty drizzle at whipping her delicate skin. This would be over soon. The threads emanating from one goassamery sliver of evidence had webbed in so many others.

Maa will be there soon...

She only thought of her Anandi. Tomorrow was her 10th birthday and she hadn't seen her for the last three years. Would Anandi still remember her maa?

Malana police and Crime Branch, Delhi, were waiting for her to make it out safely before striking. It would all end now. The rituals, the deaths...

She felt the sharp sting on her thigh and fell headlong, the prickly bramble piercing her arms.

Gasping, she looked up and saw the blurred images dancing like they often did during the rituals and in her nightmares. The cremation ash smeared on their bodies reeked of their sins known to all and yet to none.

Anandi, It's your responsibility now, dear.

He came forward and grasping the unruly locks of her disarrayed hair, tugged it behind even as she screamed in agony and she could see the tiny skull tattoo carved on his elbow... like the others assembled there.

Fear engulfed her like never before.

"Hand it over" He bellowed.

"Rot...in...hell..." she muttered.

He raised his hand holding his sickle.

Maa loves you, darling.

12 years later

The milk swelling up to a boil beckoned Anandi even as soft chuckling Shimla rain clattered on her kitchen parapet. Shimla was always home.

She loved the fog-filled misty daybreaks, but that morning anxiety clung to her like a second skin.

She hadn't heard from Shankar in the last three days since he had left for one of his secret rendezvous. She had stopped asking him ages ago. She knew it wasn't any other woman, her radar never betrayed her. Even their year-old son Aatman's cherubic chatter didn't entice him anymore.

Shankar Chaudhary and Anandi had met in college and fallen in love. He was her senior by a couple of years.

Anandi had lost her only living parent, her father when she was barely 18 and Shankar became the anchor she always yearned for. For once somebody understood her. He had supported her and encouraged her to move back to Shimla last year despite him having a lucrative career in Delhi. She now lived in her childhood home amidst her parents' belongings and memories.

All was well in the first month after their move but one day the house had been ransacked thoroughly when they were out. Police investigation didn't result in anything conclusive. Anandi would have let it go but the incident occurred twice in the last 9 months.

After the last time it happened Shankar had left for his 'office' work and had disappeared.

"Shankar, where are you...?" She spoke to the open window as the rains reduced to staccato drops. "...Aatman misses you."

Clutching her sacred thread, she realised Shankar had always been an enigma. Especially the story behind the skull tattoo on his right elbow, that he never revealed to her.

She was lost in thoughts when she received a call from the local police station.

"Mrs. Chaudhary, we have a found a body on the banks of the Beas and suspect it is Mr. Shankar Chaudhary... skull tattoo..."

Anandi was distraught. Her life had come crashing down for the third time in 15 years. It began with her police-officer-mother leaving her when she was barely 7, only to surface three years later near the Malana valley, dead under mysterious circumstances. Her father had resorted to alcohol to drown his sorrows till one day the amber liquid claimed him.

It was three months after Shankar's body was discovered. Anandi missed him , his humour-laced banter, his favourite 'Black-Jack' citrus scent, his coquettish bedroom antics that bewitched her aplenty... In the past year, she had been busy multitasking, to notice anything uncanny.

Moving towards the study she picked up the envelope containing the letter from Crime Branch Delhi. There were officially closing the case dealing with her mother.

Providence had played its cards. Anandi decided to visit Malana.

Vivaan would finally meet his paternal grandparents who were based in Malana and had never met them since they disliked her for Shankar. She would get her closure too.

With an anxiety ridden heart she packed up everything belonging to Aatman and her and also a framed photo of her mother with her, taken just before she had disappeared. Her mother's office had sent a box of her belongings after her death. While most of them were files containing case documents which were done with, this photo frame was what caught Anandi's attention, as if it wanted to speak to her. The ornate ceramic frame formed a huge section leaving little space for the small photo. Anandi had kept it with her ever since.

The rickety state-transport bus chugged into a lazy Malana town-street. Under the sanguine daybreak the bus-station seemed antiquated in the absence of enthusiastic travellers. As Anandi alighted with a sleeping Aatman strapped to the carrier, dragging her luggage, the soft draft sent a chill down her spine.

That no one except the office knew she was here wasn't enough to alleviate the disquietude imprinted upon her psyche.

"New, Madam? Welcome Malana." She was startled and turned to see a cycle-rickshaw. The balding elderly driver's pan-stained teeth matched his dhoti* but at the moment he was God sent.

"Thank you, kaka. I want to go to..." She had to stay at some B&B since no one knew her here. An idea struck right then.

"Um... kaka, do you know the Chaudhary residence? My father-in-law is a plantation owner." She crossed her fingers.

"You are...?" Kaka looked shocked. "... the daughter-in-law? Why didn't you tell me earlier? Let's go."

Soon the rumpty rickshaw wailed its way out of the acuminated pathway.

The breeze softly patted her face as the septuagenarian kaka wouldn't stop talking about the Chaudharys. Anandi couldn't let go the premonitive chills gradually cementing their place in her heart.

The cycle-rickshaw entered a cul-de-sac under a huge canopy of bougainvillea creepers, lined with marigold bushes. The security guards at the gate seemed to know Dagdu kaka and even waved a greeting. The rickshaw screeched and halted at the entrance of a massive bungalow. The lone structure comprising of finest architecture was surrounded by lush greenery. The rising and falling tree covers in their denseness raised her ethereal spirits.

Aatman began to wail right then.

"What is this ruckus?" A deep baritone sounded behind her instantly quietening Aatman.

"BHAUSAAB" Kaka rushed towards the tall man, in a spotless dhotar-kurta probably in his sixties with lush grey hair aristocratically combed backward, with a rugged face and stern eyes that slit and bored into her soul.

"Koun hai*?" A harried woman in a starched cotton saree rushed outside. Anandi gasped. The woman had Shankar's attractive brown orbs.

Kaka made the introductions and there was a stunned silence.

"Why are you here? Where is Shankar?" Bhausaab asked unperturbed.

All mayhem broke lose as Anandi revealed the truth about her husband but Aatman's presence seemed to work as a balm for the distraught parents.

"Anandi beta..." Bhausaaeb spoke later. "...our relationship didn't begin well. But let bygones be. Aatman is our blood. Please stay with us."

Anandi's heart soared in delight. Now all she needed was a post-box number to forward her mail.

Later that night as she slept with Aatman next to her, she felt a presence in her bedroom. She woke up with a start switching on the night lamp but there was no one.

Only a mild whiff of a lingering citrus fragrance....

Black-Jack

The Malana post-office was ill-equipped, unlike Mumbai. But the limited staff was efficient and rushed to help her more so because of her surname. The Chaudharys lived away from the town close to the valley and her father-in-law had arranged for her transport that needed crossing the tough terrain.

"Beta..." her mother-in-law said that evening. "...we couldn't do the rituals for newlyweds, but our family has a tradition. We are Shiv-bhakts. Every night we have a ritual, followed by the Mahapuja on the full moon night. Tonight, we would like Aatman and you to join us."

"What puja is it, Maasaab?".

"We worship Shiva at Nandi-Dwaar, behind the bungalow. Aghori babas come over to perform the rituals."

That night holding a struggling Aatman, as Anandi approached a cavern-like structure lit by torches; she saw a wooden bull-head embellishing the entrance. A group of people were gathered around a bon-fire. Her in-laws, seated on the high chair near a fire pit, presided over the proceedings.

Several men in semi-nude state had white powder smeared on their bodies and face, with a bright blood red tilak adorning the foreheads, danced around the bonfire. Their mat of unruly hair was tied up on their heads in a ragged bun. All of them had the skull tattoo near their right elbows, like Shanker. They held 'skulls' and were chanting hymns...

What kind of ritual was this?

She was rooted to her spot despite Aatman wriggling in her arms. Amidst the olfactory overload she got the unmistaken whiff of the overfamiliar Black-Jack citrus fragrance. Chaos prevailed in her fudged mind.

After a while, everyone stood up and the chanting stopped and the crowd soon disappeared

Anandi had read about the Aghori cults and ominously realised the powder was cremation ash.

That night when she returned to her room, she felt someone had been through her things. She couldn't point to anything specific though. Something wasn't right. What were the Aghoris doing here in a place where even tourists were banned, instead of a crematorium?

Her mother had died here. Would these people know anything about that murder that remained unresolved to date? Her mother was working undercover when she passed. The details were classified. Her father had never favoured her mother's dangerous job liaisons and stayed away from anything that reminded him of his wife.

She had to find out. She opened her laptop and clicked away into the secret folder where she had all scanned copied of the police reports and newspaper archives. During her weekly visit to the post-office and the bank she had enquired subtly with a couple of old timers but they seemed to know nothing about the murder case that had shaken the valley. There was no way to find out the truth without raising red flags.

She couldn't ask her father-in-law given what she had witnessed the last few nights.

The following morning, she received a text message from a private number.

'Stay away... else join your mother'

That night Anandi didn't want to attend the creepy ritual. She was wondering about her excuse when her eyes fell on the photo frame. She walked towards the showcase and took out the frame.

"What did you find out maa....?" She spoke as her eyes filled. "...I am all alone here. But how can I get to the truth maa...? Should I just leave this place? It scares me..."

Right then Aatman crawled to the edge of the bed and she dropped the frame on the hard floor in an attempt to hold the child from falling off the bed. She placed him with his favourite toy in the centre of the bed and moved to clear the floor of the glass from the shattered frame. But as she picked up the frame it gave away and broke into two halves right in the centre opening some kind of a cavity. She widened it further... it crumbled and a chip fell out of the crevice. She held it up and wondered what this was all about... was it something her mother wanted her to have?

She had to check. From what she remembered, her mother was technically sound, far ahead of her times.

Feigning a headache, she sent Aatman ahead and tried to fit the chip into the laptop's chip holder. Fortunately, it fit and covering herself with a thick blanket she began to observe her screen...

The video was grainy probably because of the formatting issues with the chip holder. Her mother was seen in a dark room with some young boys. The staccato of her voice wasn't intelligible but Anandi could make out words like 'stupor', 'Dazed', 'Hallucinations', 'brainwashed' 'Meth' etc. The video further revealed a small unit where a few men smeared with ash were sprawled while others scrapped out the powder and packed them in tiny pouches. The Aghoris seemed to be in a delirium... It was then it was revealed, those pouches contained drugs and these men weren't Aghoris at all. They were all carriers for the drug mafia...

The video went blank after her mother revealed a locker number with the concrete evidence.

Was Shanker too a part of this charade? Anandi shivered beneath the blanket.

Anandi emailed the information about the locker number and other details she found to the Crime Branch, Delhi. She knew a couple of officers who had been in touch with her all these years enquiring about her well-being. She knew the following night had the full moon in its radiant glory and beneath the garb of the ritual, drugs dealings would materialise. She had to escape this god forbidden place with Aatman as soon as possible.

But the terrain was impossible to cross without help and her father-in-law would know immediately. As she pondered with her heart pacing, she realised the break-ins at her home were because of this chip. The photo had been staring at all of them all the time but no one took any notice.

The next day passed in a blur and in the evening, just as she packed her bags ready to leave, her bedroom door was kicked open scaring Aatman, and two burly men barged inside along with her father-in-law.

"Search every nook and corner. Rip her luggage apart if needed..." The patriarch bellowed even as Maasaab took away a wailing Aatman to Anandi's horror.

They didn't find anything.

"Look Anandi, I have nothing against you. I never did. Else you wouldn't have just got a warning. I only want what your mother left for you. I know you have it."

"I... I don't know what you are talking about..." Anandi trembled in fear.

"Cut the crap. I am not Shankar. My spineless son fell for you forgetting the very purpose of his mission...." Anandi gasped as he continued. "...I didn't let my son betray me and will not let anyone else do it. You mother backstabbed my people. She was to report us... I couldn't do that. This is our bread and butter..."

"...STOP STOP..." Anandi screamed. "...You are criminals. You are ruining young lives... Aghori's of all the people?"

She felt the sting on her cheek as he slapped her.

"You shall remain in this room till you hand over the evidence to us." The man declared and walked out of the room.

She remained in a fetal position sobbing late into the night when she heard a scrape and click.

The door opened even as she gasped and a shadow walked in. Before she could react a hard hand covered her mouth and she didn't need light to know who it was, as the citrus fragrance gushed into her nostrils.

"Shhh... Anandi be quiet. We have to run away, but we have to get Aatman first." Shankar's whispered.

Anandi couldn't stop the rush of tears meandering their way along her cheeks.

"What... what is all this Shankar...?"

"Long story short Anandi, I despised what my family did yet I couldn't escape. Then I was assigned to trap you into marriage and get the evidence, but I fell in love. For the first time I felt human and not a commodity. I thought these people would let me be but... I had to give myself up else they would have harmed you. But looks like they managed to get you here...I am sorry Anandi... for everything..." Shanker held her close. She gripped at his jacket sleeves as if it was the last thread of hope.

"What do we do now, Shanker?" She asked.

"I need the evidence, Anandi. I saw you here and was shocked... but I have arranged for the Crime Branch to raid here tonight and catch them red handed. It took me over a year to plan this. Tonight, it is... Anandi." Shanker was breathing heavily.

Anandi trusted Shanker at that moment and handed over the chip she had hidden in her undergarment. Shankar hid it in his jacket and used his mobile to text something. His mobile buzzed again. He read the message and grasped her hand.

"Anandi, they are here. Come on we have to take Aatman. Its show time."

What followed was a sudden sweep of law enforcement officers as the stunned Aghoris and those gathered for the culmination of the ritual grappled in the dark. Shanker snatched Aatman from his shocked mother and rushed towards Anandi.

"Take him and run towards the bike marked 9. It belongs to the Crime Branch operation in-charge. He will take you to safety. And Anandi... I love you. Always."

Anandi was tongue tied and she did as told. As the bike moved away from the cacophony of screams, she couldn't see Shanker anymore.

Epilogue

Two years later

Shimla

Anandi woke up to the vibrating alarm and stretched. She turned towards the sound of the rains lashing at the bedroom window. She smiled and turned to look at the sleeping Atman.

Two years ago, she hadn't expected this end. Despite all that transpired and multiple court visits, Shanker and she stood by each other. Shanker was a crucial eye witness and had to serve a small jail time despite the verdict being in their favour overall.

She got up to prepare lunch. Shanker was waiting for their weekly visit.

CHAPTER THREE

SACRAMENT 1.05 - THE UNSEXY OCCULT

By Kitiera Morey

The envoy flipped a page in the tiny notebook held in her right hand. Her eyes (hidden behind dark sunglasses to protect her fragile pupils from the glaring sun above) never left Ramohella's face as she recited, "Your feeding may not result in a kill."

Ramohella leaned against the door frame of Sacrament's (her salon, whose name had angered many Others and humans, much to her delight) open back door. It wasn't comfortable, yet she had to feel a million times better than the vampiric envoy before her. While she couldn't taste the vampire's emotions (of course The Forgathering would send an Archetype to speak to her), she knew standing in the sun hurt. The envoy wore layered clothing despite the time of year, kept her (stereotypical) long dark hair around her face, and if her skin wasn't slathered with a spelled sunscreen, Ramohella would snort a bottle of hair dye.

But all those precautions did was keep the vampire from death. They did nothing to minimize the pain daylight caused.

As owner of the building, manners dictated Ramohella invite the envoy into her salon. But it wasn't often she had the upper hand on a member of The Forgathering. Yes, the vampire wasn't much more than a hired goon with little power inside the organization, yet it was as close as Ramohella would get. Gods forbid the lead members do more than judge and bark orders from their gilded perches.

"I have to wonder if this reminder is a...courtesy for you, too? Have you been a naughty girl?"

The envoy's jaw tightened; a gesture Ramohella would have missed had she not been studying the vampire so closely.

"Archetypes have self-control."

"Do you now?" Ramohella laughed. "Then I must have heard some rumors incorrectly."

Long fingers crushed the notebook. A low, feral growl followed.

Ramohella's laugh deepened. Either the Archetype was young and still believed the sickeningly perfect image her people projected, or she was old enough to know the truth and clung to the lie to maintain the power the Archetypes wielded. Whichever was the case, to have an Other such as Ramohella—a lowly wraith—hint at reality was a greater insult than if Ramohella had dosed the vampire in holy water.

Was it wise of her to poke at the envoy?

On the list of stupid things Ramohella could do, giving The Forgathering any reason to dislike her more than they did ranked pretty high. Yet she refused to let them think they had her completely cowed. That wasn't the way of a wraith. Even if Ramohella acted unconventional in practically every other way, she could never rid herself of the noteworthy steeled pride at every wraith's core.

The envoy's top lip curled. "How many decades have you lived? Shouldn't all these years have taught you not to listen to foolish lies?"

Ramohella shrugged. "That would suck all the fun out of life."

The envoy flinched at the word 'suck'.

Ramohella rolled her eyes. The Archetypes were so prissy. Even though they still had canines meant for ripping open the veins of their victims, and the urge to hunt still flooded them whenever the thirst grew strong (even if they denied it), they tried to distinguish themselves from the Bloodbornes (made vampires) by abandoning all language that alluded to their darker natures. Their haughty air resembled the royal humans that projected importance by crafting an infallible demeanor the 'common folk' could never achieve.

The thought of humans made Ramohella glance at the watch she wore. She swore under her breath. As much as she enjoyed this pointless pestering, it'd eaten into her time. Now she had less than a half hour to finish preparing before her special client came in for her appointment.

"You need to go," Ramohella said as she reached for her door.

"Excuse me? I don't think we're finished here."

"It's pretty simple. I can't murder the human. I've been doing this longer than you've existed, and I've mastered my technique. Don't worry. Unless something goes horribly wrong, we won't see each other again."

"But—"

Ramohella slammed the door in the envoy's face. A string of expletives followed, but that was the most the vampire could do. As long as Ramohella remained in the salon, she was untouchable. Unless the envoy called for backup, but it likely wouldn't come. It wasn't against the law to be rude. Many of The Forgathering's laws were ridiculous, but none sunk that low.

Sacrament wasn't a large building. Its quaint size aided the charming air Ramohella had established. She could have gone for a more cliched atmosphere akin to her nature, but while she felt no shame at being a wraith, she didn't want her place of work to drip with reminders of it. She doubted it'd alert any of the humans in town to the truth about her, but she was more than a wraith even if many Others didn't treat her so. Even those of her own species couldn't understand why she lived as she did.

Actually, every other wraith thought her insane. To exist so close to humans, Ramohella had agreed to only feed every three months. To go any longer would leave her a raging mess that could ravage the small town she inhabited. It was a risk, but she'd made it work for the past forty years.

Plus, Ramohella didn't wholly adhere to The Forgathering's conditions. She'd had a witch spell several of the art pieces that hung in the main room of the salon to harvest the lesser negative emotions her clients and employees gave off daily. If Ramohella touched the pieces, the emotions they'd gathered would help restore a bit of her energy. It was never enough to satisfy, but it kept her levelheaded.

For as odd as it may be, Ramohella loved working with hair. She would have preferred to work on Others, but none had ever sought her services. Though her reputation was the best in the tri-state area, and celebrities fought for appointments, non-humans didn't trust her. Others clung to their prejudices as if they'd cease to exist without them.

Maybe one day they'd realize what they were missing. Until then, to Hell with them. She'd continue her craft on humans, even if it was less fun.

After entering the main room, Ramohella checked that each of the eight styling stations' mirrors was covered with the black translucent silk she used when she fed. Had this been any other booked client, the mirror coverings would have been solid black silk. Unlike the average human, Ramohella needed her victim to catch glimpses of her true hideous form; to build fear—the tastiest, most filling of emotions. The longer she could draw out the moment before she revealed her actual appearance, the more satisfied she'd be (and the less likely she was to fully drain the human of all its energy).

To aid the buildup and decrease the chances of causing a heart attack, Ramohella drugged the human. The sedative wasn't strong enough to knock the human unconscious, but it helped at the end of the feeding session when she lied that all they'd seen was a dream.

Ramohella hid the sharp taste of the drug in a heady wine she served in a golden goblet encrusted with raw, priceless gems that she used with every one of her clients. To have Ramohella tend to one's hair was the height of luxury, and the wraith put out all the stops to deliver on her carefully curated fame.

If this was a typical client, Ramohella would have also served imported cheeses and meats and truffles she had made in Switzerland. But fear was harder to cultivate when a human was full (and sober). Plus, Ramohella was in no mood to clean up vomit. As it was, she expected to be scrubbing piss out of the styling chair most of the afternoon.

As always, Ramohella checked that the salon's frosted storefront window would reveal nothing of what was about to transpire. While any human glancing in would likely only see the client in the styling chair and Ramohella beside her (nothing out of the ordinary there), the wraith couldn't be sure they wouldn't glimpse her real appearance in a mirror. They probably wouldn't believe their own eyes (as humans were prone to do), but it was a risk Ramohella wasn't willing to take.

To avoid all this, the wisest choice was to feed in a more private setting. Ramohella had petitioned The Forgathering for such a place, but they'd denied her request. They felt if she jeopardized all her hard work, she was less likely to kill. Ramohella hated how right they were.

Though, unlike most wraiths, Ramohella had never enjoyed killing the handful of humans she had in her youth. She'd only done so because that was how she'd learned to feed, but it had never felt right.

And not because she was a human sympathizer. They were such obnoxious, egotistical creatures for not knowing what really happened around them. All deserved what they got when they stuck their noses in Others' business.

But killing them during feeding was wasteful. For all their faults, the intensity and spectrum of flavors of their emotions was incredible. And those tastes got better the more their suspicions rose. Even their positive emotions were a treat, even if they weren't what a wraith needed to survive.

Sanctuary lamps Ramohella had had gathered from a condemned church years ago hung from the ceiling. Most didn't know, including her employees, that the candles inside the lamps were real. Those, too, had come from the church, though Ramohella had had the blessings removed.

While a chore, Ramohella lit every candle in the ten sanctuary lamps. They provided the perfect mood lighting for the feeding to come. She also liked how their very presence caused humans who knew of their significance to froth at the mouth. Several angry churchgoers had made it a point to tell her how she spit in the face of their god.

The ceremony of all Ramohella did heightened her anticipation, so much so that her fingers shook as she lit a candle. She cursed herself when she fumbled with the match and the flame licked her thumb. She forced herself to calm before she struck another match and finished her task.

Done, Ramohella took care of the ladder she'd been using, and had just enough time to ready the goblet of wine and stand behind the check-in counter before her meal arrived. The victim was Deborah Wilson, the mayor's wife, and the town's biggest gossip. Ramohella didn't think the woman had ever been happy a day in her fifty-two years of life, and Deborah made that everyone else's problem. The mood of a room instantly darkened whenever the woman entered, which made her the perfect choice for a feeding.

Was it more satisfying to break a cheerful, good-natured human?

Yes, the negative emotions were sweeter and left Ramohella with a euphoric high that lasted weeks. But she only did this once a year, on the anniversary of Sacrament's opening. To have multiple humans' demeanors change so drastically every year would draw too much attention. Ramohella doubted the humans would figure out her secret, but they were amazing at creating vicious rumors that could cripple a business overnight.

Deborah becoming more sour and unlikeable over the next few days wouldn't make anyone bat an eyelash. They'd just think she'd discovered her husband's newest mistress or maybe her last liposuction treatment hadn't gone as planned.

As soon as Deborah stormed through the door, the acidic tang of her irritation filled Ramohella's mouth. Instead of ignoring it like she'd do on any other day, she swallowed the emotion. To do so caused Deborah's irritation to spike higher. Her pulse had likely quickened, and she wiped her palms against her dark blue pencil skirt as she neared the counter.

"No need to tell me and make this headache worse. I know I'm a few minutes late," Deborah huffed. "My damn son woke me up at three this morning, shit-faced, and demanded I come get him. Little bastard was at Jimmy Allbars' house, all the way in Clymer. Do you know how far of a drive that is?"

Ramohella stared at Deborah, wondering if the question was rhetorical. With a woman like her, it was hard to tell.

On the off-chance it wasn't, Ramohella chose not to answer. Instead, she gave Deborah the same blank, uninterested stare she'd given the vampiric envoy when she'd first arrived.

Of course, Deborah noticed. And just like Ramohella had wanted, it drove the woman's annoyance to new heights.

Ramohella's stomach growled, and she licked her lips. Oh, yes, she'd picked the right human.

"Is there a problem with me being late?"

"I require my clients to arrive on time. I'm extremely busy, you know."

Deborah crossed her arms under her breasts. "If you're refusing the appointment because I came in a little after ten, then I demand my deposit back. Five minutes is nothing. What if the weather was bad? Or a road accident had happened?"

"But neither one of those scenarios is the case. You just overslept because your son is...ill-mannered."

Bright red splotches bloomed in Deborah's cheeks. Her instant rage coated Ramohella's tongue, and she imagined it was as tasty as a well-prepared steak was for a human. It wasn't a five-course dinner at the fanciest restaurant, but Deborah's anger still brought a smile to Ramohella's face.

The smile cut through Deborah's anger, though it brought no positive feeling. "So, are you still going through with the appointment?"

Ramohella sighed after letting a long moment of silence pass. "I suppose I can make an exception for the mayor's wife."

Deborah's following grin was that of a spoiled, entitled child. And the syrupy sweet taste of that rottenness made Ramohella's head swim.

"Well...thanks."

Ramohella gestured to the goblet. "Please enjoy this complimentary wine. I guarantee your nerves will unravel after the first few sips."

Deborah snatched the goblet. "This is more like what I paid for."

Though her appearance was that of a high-class lady, Deborah chugged the wine like her son had probably done the previous night. Ramohella cursed under her breath. The sedative wouldn't take effect instantly, but it was fast-acting. Usually it kicked in after she'd shampooed the victim's hair and started on the cut (yes, Ramohella styled the hair. She had an image to uphold), and it fully immobilized the victim and made their thoughts fuzzy by the time she finished.

But that was when the wine was sipped.

Ramohella would have to skip the first few steps of the process if she intended to get Deborah's hair done before she fed. While she was loving the constant stream of impatience to suckle on, she would have preferred to stick to her plan.

As quickly as she'd grabbed the goblet, it tumbled from Deborah's hand. The loud, unexpected clang that followed made Ramohella jump. What remained of the wine splattered the floor, counter, and Deborah's shoes.

"Wha—"

Deborah's eyes rolled into the back of her skull just before she collapsed to the floor. Her thin body convulsed on the hard tile; her head smacking with sickening thuds.

Surprise kept Ramohella rooted in place. What was going on? The drug hadn't had enough time to work, and even if it had, no human had ever reacted this way.

Could Deborah be on something that could negatively interact with the sedative? But that couldn't be the case. Ramohella had done her research. The most Deborah abused was alcohol, and she hit up a pot dealer once in a while.

Neither one of those substances had been in her system when she'd arrived, though. The mayor's wife was far from a good woman, but she never drove intoxicated. She'd lost her sister to a drunk driver and pushed for harsh punishment for those that got behind the wheel of a car when not sober. If she could hang each person who got a DUI, she would.

So what caused this seizure?

Standing around like an idiot wouldn't bring the answer, but Ramohella wasn't sure what to do, having never dealt with a serious medical emergency. The most logical thing was to clear the space around Deborah, so she was less likely to injure herself more than she already had.

This Ramohella did.

As she finished, Deborah stopped moving. Not even her chest moved.

"You'd better not be dead."

Ramohella kneeled by the woman and felt at different pulse points. No heartbeat.

"F**k."

In a flash, Ramohella crossed the main room; her goal was the back door. She wrenched it open, and as assumed, the envoy was still in the alley. She'd found shade, though, and was playing on her phone.

At the sound of the door opening, the vampire looked up. "Your feeding can't be over yet."

"Death has a way of cutting that short."

The envoy's back straightened. "Excuse me?"

Ramohella held up a hand. "Calm down. I did nothing. She just had a seizure and died."

"A seizure because you took it too far."

"Don't believe me? Come in and check for yourself."

Like a bullet, the envoy ran through the alley and pushed past Ramohella. The wraith rolled her eyes, closed the door, and followed. By the time she returned to the main room, the envoy had finished her examination of Deborah.

"So?" Ramohella asked.

The envoy frowned. "You...did nothing wrong. A brain aneurysm took her."

"Why not try sounding more disappointed?"

"I just—This is unexpected."

"You're telling me. I now have a dead body on my hands, and I'm still hungry."

The envoy smirked. "Don't forget the time crunch."

Though smug, the vampire was right. Ramohella had until midnight to feed. But she would not do it alone.

"Well, guess who gets to help?"

CHAPTER FOUR

THE SHIROYAMA RITUAL

By Aboli Mane

Wintry winds eddied along the narrow pathways blanketed in white. In Shiroyama village clustered into the bosom of the ice-capped ranges a hub-hub arose in the late afternoon. From her perch, at the entryway of the shack, Yuki could see the trail that swept around the mountain like a silver thread. The procession of villagers carried bright blue paper lanterns making their way up the trail. Straw boots marred the freshly fallen snow.

"Here you go." Mama finally allowed her a glimpse in the mirror. Yuki stared into the small oval at her pale reflection. Her hair as dark as a raven's feather fell in straight wisps about her delicate shoulders. Two brown eyes twinkling with excitement. Rosy lips pursed nervously. Yuki had turned thirteen the previous month. The reason for her excitement was obvious. She rocked on the new straw boots Papa had made for her.

THE SELECTION OF A SACRED STRAWBERRY

The family was dressed in their heaviest winter kimonos, layers upon layers of linen topped with dark silk. Careful as not to drop the precious mirror, Yuki handed it back to Mama. Her brother, Tori sulked at the threshold. Snot-nosed with bristly hair and a delicate disposition, he would be staying in the main shrine as everyone else attended the Kaidan. That was what the head priest Mikoto had declared.

"I wanted to listen to the stories." Tori's voice was plugged up by the cold. The rare medicine man that visited this misty village had said he'd suffer during the cold season. It had been a little disappointing to Yuki, for she loved to frolic in duvet snow. Yuki had to content herself by playing with Sayuri or Akihito, which was annoying at times because both caught the flu too easily. Yuki on the other hand never felt the cold.

Mama and Papa often teased her that this was because she was named after the snow.

"I'm sorry Tori. When you've grown tall next few moons, you'll be able to come." Yuki watched as Mama caressed Tori's hair. "And I'll be able to take you to the fields with me for the harvest." Papa declared tightening his straw boots. Tori protested this. The Kaidan was an important tradition that the settlers in Shiroyama performed on the New Moon that fell on the darkest night of Winter every thirteen years.

The oldest legend of Shiroyama spoke of the deity defeating a hundred ghosts to make the mountain free of supernatural influence. Thus retelling the tale of the ghosts was a way to honor the guardian.

The family set out of their home, a moderate-sized hut close to the terraced fields where they grew rice. Outsiders often wondered how Shiroyama came to sufficiency, how every year despite other areas coming to misfortune, it managed a plentiful harvest.

To such curiosities, Mikoto the head priest of the mountain shrine would laugh and say over a cup of sake at the village inn. "The deity is merciful. An offering every thirteen years is the secret." The patrons would laugh along.

Yuki did not know the full tale, but she was thankful. The diety ensured the people would stay close to home and not wander all the way to the capital for work. Smiling, she looked forward to hearing the other stories for the first time.

Tori carried the blue paper lantern as he walked beside Yuki. "Look sis, a bird!" Yuki giggled. Tori liked birds since that was what his name meant. A fat sparrow perched itself on a spruce letting out a delightful little warble. "Sparrow!"

By the time Tori had finished pointing at all the tiny birds that flitted in the vicinity, the Yamada family joined them. Yuki waved to Sayuri and Akihito. The children quickly formed a group and dashed before the elders.

Akihito and Tori ran a short race, where Akihito purposely tripped, falling face first into a large snow drift. When they saw his face caked with white they all collapsed with laughter. Snow and gravel crushed under her straw boots.

"I brought a bunch of nuts and crude sugar. Let's share!" Sayuri patted her belt. "Me first! Me first!" Tori snatched at her belt. By the time the vermillion shrine gates peeped from among the blanketed spruces they had left their parents far behind and finished all the snacks.

The ascent to the shrine and the grounds on the sacred mountain was arduous. The stone lanterns at the base flickered with flames, driving the chill away. The carved dog guardians on either side of the stairway were covered in snow. A line of smaller lanterns dotted their path ahead, dwindling into the fog that arose from Shiroyama.

"Let's wait." Akihito sat down on a step. "You've rehearsed the story you're going to tell, right?." "Yeah, you know the one." Yuki answered.

"The Story of the Snow Sister. I'm glad Tori is not able to attend, you're already half a ghost with that name." Akihito joked. Yuki wanted to hit him, but she thought the better. Once they were older and married she could hit him as much as she wanted.

"Play kagome kagome!" Tori tugged at Sayuri's red-ribboned plaits jumping up and down. His favorite game. Singing a song, children linked arms and revolved around a child that sat with his eyes covered in the circle. When the song stopped the child in the circle had to guess who stood behind his back. If he guessed correctly, he could switch places with the other.

"Alright, little monkey. We will play." Akihito traced a circle in the snow. Tori shrunk to his haunches and covered his eyes with his palms. Akihito, Sayuri and Yuki held hands and began the age-old rhyme.

Kagome Kagome,
O bird in the cage,
When will you come out?
Neither dawn nor night,
The crane and turtle fall,
Who stands behind you now?

As the song stopped, Tori answered.

"Sayuri." Sayuri made a face and replaced Tori. The game spanned many rounds until the three teens grew bored.

"It's not fair that Tori is always able to guess correctly!" Sayuri groused.

"That's because there's only three of us. If there were more...the little monkey would be confused." Akihito teased. Tori stuck out his tongue. "You're jealous because I always win!" He remarked petulantly. Footsteps. Ah, here were the adults!

"Tori, why don't you ride on my shoulders? I and Uncle Yamada shall take turns bringing you to the top." Papa hoisted Tori as he squealed in delight. The men tramped ahead. The shrine steps grew slippery due to the ice, so one had to be careful. Mama and Aunt Yamada seemed to be in a hurry.

Yuki had to run to catch up with them.

"Kikyo, you remember the last time?" Aunt Yamada spoke in such a hush that her voice seemed to emanate from the sky. "Yeah. Furogami's son..." Mama gulped. Furogami? Yuki did not know any family by that name. "They left soon after, didn't they?" Aunt Yamada went on.

"Yes. Their son got lost in the mountain, lured by a blue light. Don't you think..." Aunt Yamada's eyes held a question that Yuki could not decipher. Mama shook her head firmly. "The boy... For the village-"

"Yuki!" Sayuri grabbed her arm. Yuki halted. Mama and Aunt Yamada jerked as though alarmed. "W-we are going ahead, do try to keep up!" They left. Yuki could only stare, what did all this mean?

"Let's go slower, I'm exhausted." Sayuri panted. Yuki nodded absently. Her head was spinning. They stopped to drink from glacial springs and pay their respects to the statues. The sight from up here was so beautiful. They could glimpse their little village cradled in the snow.

Deep in the crevasses of the mountain a blue light danced amidst the rocks. Yuki stared, entranced. It was as though the light was calling to her. Whispering her name.

"Yuki. Yuki. Yuki..."

"Yuki!" Sayuri shook her hard. "Come on!" Absolutely spooked, Yuki picked the hem of their kimono and dashed upward the steps.

Crushing shriveled persimmons and chestnuts they ran until the second gate of the shrine, red and imposing, yet a symbol of safety for anyone that saw it, became visible in the fog.

Once inside, they hurried across the vast stone courtyard. Ice cold mush had seeped into Yuki's white socks. The main shrine rose like an ancient warrior, the ebony slats curving onto a gabled roof. All the dark wood in its construction was from a sacred grove. The screens and transoms were egg white, standing out against the rest of the structure. Massive stone lanterns threw restless shadows across the ground. Yuki and Sayuri halted near the shrine, panting heavily.

"Was that real?" Yuki whispered. Her eyes were wide and staring. "What was it?" Sayuri blurted in confusion. Yuki blinked, deciding what to say. Some things on Shiroyama were unexplainable. "A blue light-"

"A blue light? You're imagining things, girl." Yuki and Sayuri turned. Tori and Mikoto stood in the entryway. A bald man with heavy eyebrows and a wrinkled face, Mikoto's expression was always sour, as though he'd sucked on a lemon. Yet now he attempted a smile. An unpleasantness arose within Yuki's throat.

"I saw it. I know what I saw." Yuki insisted.

"I've been on the mountain far longer than you, there are no such lights. Don't frighten your friend." Mikoto laughed. Sayuri tried to tug her backward.

"Sis! Look what I got!" Tori showed off a wooden crane and turtle. The toys slipped from his hands and came bouncing down the wooden platform. Yuki instantly picked them up.

"That's very lucky." Outloud it sounded as though she was trying to convince herself. The crane and turtle were symbols of long life. Their fall was considered an ill omen. "Mikoto said he will give me a tour of the shrine. Isn't that nice?" Tori beamed. Yuki glared at Mikoto.

"I've spoken to your parents. Don't worry, everything is as arranged." The priest patted Yuki's head. Yuki flinched, sensing that there was something that she did not know.

"Come back soon, sis!" Tori grinned.

In the massive darkened chamber within the furthest premises of the shrine Yuki huddled closer to Sayuri and Akihito. The villagers conversed in whispers but Yuki kept shifting.

Why did she not know anything about the Furogami's? Why was Mama so tense? Who had she been speaking of? What was that blue light that Mikoto said he'd never seen? The village that she had lived in all her life, why did it seem as though it was keeping secrets? Mama had not spoken to her. Nor had Papa.

Mikoto believed that this three roomed chamber was right at the border of the spirit world. The rooms were arranged in a straight line. The screen to the last room was shut and only the blue glow of a hundred lanterns flickered through the rice paper screen. Mikoto's underling spoke in a strangely haunting hymn, outlining the rules of the game.

"The ritual will go on through the night. Each shall tell a weird tale. Each must at the end of your narration get up from this room, extinguish the flame of a lantern, stare at your face in the mirror and return. You cannot pause your story. You cannot refuse to enter the room. The lucky one will see something special. Mikoto-sama shall be in the shrine preparing the offering. No one must leave the chamber."

Nobody spoke. Yuki's heart thudded violently. A breeze rattled the screen doors, making the lanterns flicker. For some reason, she wanted to stop this ritual.

"Begin."

With a rustle of his robes, the underling left. Nobody dared to speak. Then her father cleared his throat. His voice sounded faint as he began the first tale. People had to duck their heads forward to listen.

"The First Ghost was the Spirit of the Lantern..."

Huddled between Sayuri and Akihito, Yuki felt consoled that she wasn't alone in this creepy room. When the tale was finished her father shuffled out. Wooden sandals clumped across the dark hallway. Everyone waited with bated breath until they heard the clogs making their way back. Father returned to his spot. In the pale bluish light, he and Mama appeared sickly.

The atmosphere grew macabre as each tale was told. With each extinguished lantern, the room seemed to close in on its occupants. As though the spirits were listening too. The shudder of every uneven slat, the creak of the wind, and every sound made Yuki's anxiety balloon. Tori, she was worried about Tori. The only images that flashed in her head were the blue light and the crane and turtle falling.

She could not discern who was actually speaking. Sayuri and Akihito got their chance. When they were done, they clung to her as though she was their crutch. Yuki wanted this to be over. A fierce wind howled, whistling through the gaps in the screens like the scream of a vengeful spirit.

Yuki startled when Sayuri poked her arm.

"It's your turn." Her voice was tiny. "The hundredth tale."

"T-The Hundredth Ghost, Sister of the Snow." It took her a moment to remember. In a cracked, wavering tone choked with fear Yuki began. "On snowy winter nights such as these she spirits children away to p-play..."

"Accompanied by child ghosts, she lures her victims into a game. Shining in a blue light..." Yuki did not move a muscle as sweat pooled across her warm panicked body. By the end, she composed herself a little. There was something vital she had realized. If she had seen the blue light... that only meant...

The hallway stood before her in sinister gloom, as though spirits with a million arms would snatch her into its depths. Yuki stood. She gathered the folds of her kimono and advanced towards the lantern room. Behind her Akihito screamed in protest. Sayuri lay limply, futilely clutching at her kimono.

Yuki found her courage. She was not just named after snow, but also after courage. In the third room, only a single lantern flickered luridly. The room was plunged into utter blackness as she extinguished it.

Yuki stumbled a little plopping right in front of the small oval mirror fixed onto the low table.

She expected to see her frightened face.

Instead she saw Tori.

"Sis. I'm stuck. Sis. They're inviting me to play." Tori's plugged up little voice stabbed like a sword through her ears. She could see it so clearly. Tori clad in a thin white shift in the dense forest of Shiroyama, lost in the blizzard. Ghostly blue children flickering around him.

"I'm stuck in the circle, Sis. I can't guess who is behind me. I-" Yuki pulled back her fist and drove her knuckles into the mirror. The shards lodged into her skin as she shrieked. She drove her fist into the mirror repeatedly until it cracked.

Then as wild as the blizzard that roared in the mountains she tore through the rice paper screens onto the bitter snow. Nobody could stop her as she sprinted past the grounds into the forest, her wet socks freezing against her feet. Sayuri and Akihito were screaming her name.

"Tori!"

Her call was smothered by the blizzard but she yelled herself hoarse.

"Take me, you monster! Take me! Leave him alone!" Hot tears stung her cheek, her arm throbbed. Crimson blood spurted from her wounds leaving a trail in the whiteness. The blizzard abated. In the midst of a clearing stood seven ethereal children. Tori, trapped in the circle, cried as soon as he saw her.

"The priest is evil! He left me in the forest! They won't let me go! I'm scared, sis!" Tears and snot streamed down his freezing face.

"It's alright." Yuki's anger had disappeared. "I'll play."

She joined the seven ghostly children. Their fingers were sculpted in snow. Poor children sacrificed to the deity, in exchange for a prosperous harvest. Poor children left to die in the cold. No blue light lured the children. It was all a plan. After all, what was the value of a child against thirteen years of prosperity?

"Kagome, Kagome..." The rhyme unfolded in strange crystalline tones, as the music played on a glass flute. Yuki followed in a hoarse voice as they revolved in a circle.

Tori covered his eyes.

O bird in the cage,
When will you come out?

Neither dawn nor night
The crane and turtle fall
Who stands behind you now?
    The circle stopped.
    Yuki stood behind him.

CHAPTER FIVE

The Longest Night in the Darkest Forest

By Anoushka Boodhna

Once upon a time, there was a young woman who lived in a cave. She had retreated to this place, so well concealed. Much time passed with her alone in this cave. The sun and the moon circled around each other many, many times.

The cave was small and mostly in the shadows. During the day, the cave was bathed fleetingly in a soft, creamy, natural light. At times when the wind was strong, it howled menacingly throughout the cave. When the rains came, the cold and damp soaked through the rock and into her body. During the winter she was frozen, and all she could think about was the sharpness of pain.

She had very few belongings. A bag and a book, which had been given to her by her grandmother. She could no longer remember her face and sometimes her heart would wail and moan. When she was sad, she would read the stories and the poetry. When the sun shone, she would take the book out of the cave and sing the songs and the chants. When the winds howled so hard that she could feel a fierce anger vibrating through her bones, she would hold the book close to her. Some days she would try to converse with her grandmother. As she could no longer remember her face, the young woman would invoke other memories. Her dewy brown eyes, the touch of her soft, papery skin, the echoless clangs of beaded woody jewellery and the musky and sweet spices of her cooking that hung in the air at her home.

One day, she awoke. Around this time of year, the winter is turning into spring. Today something was different. She had a dream and saw a sky, mottled with clouds, and a bright almost white light radiating from something that could be either the sun or the moon. She had been dancing in the sky and the clouds had peeled away like paper and revealed the brilliance of a clear light blue morning being gently lit by an arriving sun. As she danced, the sky had intensified into an oceanic azure blue and she had felt a soft weight of something incredibly comforting on her chest.

Over the next few days, the memory of the vision had lingered. But, the young woman's body protested. She could no longer bear it. The jarring cramps in her feet and legs, the weariness in her young back, and the itchy eyes and scratchy throat as if assaulted by shards of glass.

Go out with the wind, she heard her grandmother say.

After so very long in this cave, she finally packed up her few belongings in the small bag and set off out of the cave. She walked further than she had ever gone before.

Within a short time, she arrived at a wooden fence on the other side of which was a deep, dark forest. She had heard the sounds of the various creatures. The more time she had spent in the cave, the surer she had become that something strange lived there too because at night, she would hear a crackling and a thudding, and a braying of something that could not be of this world.

She found the gate, pushed it open and stepped through. Closing it behind her, she sought the path into the forest. A narrow gravel path of grey pebbles that was the width of her small foot. Once she had located it, she glanced back at the cave, her home for so long, now, empty, uninhabited. She turned to look at the forest ahead of her.

The hairs of her neck stood on end. Could she hear it? That faint crackling, thudding, and braying of something strange, and not quite of this world. A shiver ran through her body. Her legs would not move. For a moment she was absolutely sure she had made the wrong decision.

Then that moment passed like a bird flapping its wings, and she was sure again that she needed to move on.

She started on her way. The forest was abundant. Big bushes. Small trees, some slim with conical heads of yellow green leaves, others squat with round heads of mossy green leaves. All swathed by grey green heart-shaped ivy on long thin vines. Patches of lush blue green ferns. A variety of grasses, some green, some furry and camel-coloured. She wondered how such wonderful things could grow out here during the winter.

She continued on. Time passed. The path widened. Taller trees emerged, silvery trunks and wispy leaves forming a narrow canopy and a greater variety of spiky and shaggy shrubbery enfolded the path. She noticed that where the pale sunlight fell, plants were coming into tiny pink and white blossoms and pretty yellow flowers had popped up on the ground. She stopped to look at them to enjoy the reflection of their golden buttery light on her fingers. A shadow passed overhead, perhaps a large bird. She looked up. Then she looked around. At that moment, she realised that she had lost her way. Perhaps some time ago now. A shiver passed through her.

Where was she? Alarmed, her mind was transported back to those cold, windy nights at the cave. Her body clenched as she remembered curling up in fear and curling around her grandmother's book.

Her eyes darted around. The forest was darkening and for some reason, the birds were no longer flying overhead. Then a crackling in the far-off background, a thudding, and a braying. A more dizzying panic arose in her mind and body and a cry from deep in her heart flooded her senses, and pushed its way into her consciousness. In the dimmed light, she suddenly realised that she was surrounded by poisonous plants with stinging hairs and ice-like thorns. Trees took on the unnerving silhouette of hooded figures with murderous sharp tools. There was no path and the forest closed in on her. She felt small, alone and helpless.

Then, a voice. A small voice that seemed to come from within her from the back of her throat and base of her neck and from her forehead all at the same time. A voice that recounted the words of her favourite poem from those days when she would read the book in the sunshine.

Touch the Earth

In harmony

Reveal your love

She knelt down, closed her eyes again and touched the earth. She felt the damp soil that was both coarse and silky. She took a breath and pulled out floral aromas from a breeze, recalling the warm, cheery glow of the yellow flowers on her fingers. As she opened her eyes, she breathed out long and steady, and right there as she watched, the leaves flip flapped away, long branches crawled back into the undergrowth and tall grass bowed to one side, almost solemnly. Revealed to her was the narrow gravel path the width of her small foot. It traced a way through the dense forest. The sky lit up and the shadows rolled away. Relieved, and grateful, she took up the path and pressed on.

Eventually, she arrived at a river. It roared. While her senses were immediately awakened by the fresh and flavoursome water, she was apprehensive. She had to cross the river. But she felt frail and her bones still ached from the time spent in the wet cave, and she was not sure that she could bear the coldness of the water. A sudden thought, she could slip and be pulled into the undertow and this became deeply upsetting to her.

In the midst of the noise of the roaring river, she caught the sound of a tinkling and trickling that was like the music of her homeland. Then a snatch of a few lyrics from one of her favourite songs from her grandmother's book came to mind.

Don't fear
Your tears
Blue lake and rocky shore
Return to me once more

She approached the bank and picked her way through some rocks. She took a tentative step onto some larger rocks. Then another step. A third. Once she was sure that they were stable enough, she ran lightly on tiptoes across to the other side of the river. Relieved, and exhausted, she sat down and let her palms fall to the ground. It was warm. After a moment, she felt better. She felt held, sure that she had felt the earth return the embrace.

Once rested, she carried on through the forest. She was surprised to find the occasional fruit hanging off a tree. Surely it was too early in the year? She ate them and found them delicious, although occasionally sour. Again, she wondered to herself how such wonderful things could grow in the winter. She continued to eat when the fruit was available. Every now and again, that strange crackling, thudding, and braying would startle her and push her on through the forest.

She walked for a long time and lost track of how long. She was not able to tell the difference between day and night because the luminosity around her in the forest was constant and the only difference was that sometimes the light had an orange tone and at other times, a silvery tone. While she could not be sure, she decided that the light was either from the sun above the canopy of the trees, or the moon.

Just as her legs were starting to feel fatigued, she arrived quite abruptly at the end of the forest where there was a gigantic slate wall. A quick scan of the wall made it clear that this wall was not for climbing. There were no obvious footholds or nooks and crags. It stretched up solidly beyond the trees.

Several thoughts ran through her mind. Should she turn back? Should she climb up? Should she seek a way around? Turning back would not take her forward and out of this forest. Besides, she had not seen any alternative paths on her way here. She could scout around and perhaps climb a tree to survey the area. But then looking up she wondered what she could possibly see through the dense forest covering. She looked around, perhaps she would find something that could help, like a large rock? Nothing.

She thought for a while about what to do. Eventually, to be sure, she settled down on the ground to touch the earth. When she opened her eyes, no leaves moved and no new path was revealed.

She looked again at the wall. She could not guess how long it would take her to climb up. It was too dangerous. If she fell and broke her leg, there would be no way to fix it and she would be trapped here forever. As if responding to her thoughts, she heard it again. The crackling, thudding, and braying of something not of this world. Facing this large wall, something pricked in her stomach.

Suddenly, there it was again, this time right behind her. She swung around. That noise. The crackling of branches, the thudding of heavy legs, and the braying sound of an enraged animal. She was trapped by this wall. Her body was trembling. A hotness emanated from her.

She swung back to face the wall and started scrambling frantically to find some kind of handhold. That failed, so she darted around looking for a bush large enough and with enough coverage to hide her.

A giant, reverberating thud. It was here!

A chilly breeze whipped her hair. Her mind cleared. She did not want to die here. She closed her eyes again. Breathing in, she brought to mind the world around her. The fragrant breeze. The golden buttery glow of flowers on her fingers. The twinkle and trickle of the water like musical notes from her homeland. The thudding was like drums and chanting. The feel of soft skin. A tiny hand curled up in hers. She breathed out and opened her eyes.

She got up to face the monster. It stared at her. She stared at it for a while.

As she watched, it changed. Eyes that seemed inhuman, yellow and sickly changed, and they were now human, lost, and tired from weeping. A body that seemed to be too large and too hairy, the hair disgusting, plastered down with grease, coarse and prickly changed too and the monster was just small and frail, sad and lonely, an unfortunate creature wearing a coat of leaves. She looked at its hands, violent with sharp claws and rock-like knuckles, painted with what could have been blood changed too and they were pink palms turned outward, open and generous and pleading.

It thudded over to her. She froze. Then, past her. Holding her breath only her eyes moved as the monster moved. The noise of crackling, thudding, and braying was deafening. The monster found a patch of ground near the wall and lay down. It turned to her and pointed a long-nailed finger in the direction that she needed to go. Up. In front of her eyes, the finger took the shape of a branch. Then, the rest of the monster transformed, slowly, into more branches, as well as roots, leaves, and bark and finally, a trunk. A soft silence. The crackling, and braying had ceased.

In place of the monster, a tall tree reached up high into the sky. A tree with a wide base and a sturdy trunk with a deep knot-hole that was hiding an owl who now looked at her quizzically. She took a few tentative steps towards the tree. She placed her hand on the trunk and closed her eyes. A faint heartbeat. The trunk was warm under her palm.

She opened her eyes. She saw that there was a way up, thick woody sinews formed a spiral bannister and beehive-like nodules formed some steps. She climbed the trunk pushing through curtains of thin, floating green yellow leaves. She went around and up and around and up. Again. And again. Time passed and her legs grew heavy. Either she was still frail from the ravages of the wet cave, or she had travelled a very long way up the tree and for a very long time. She could no longer be sure.

She was tremendously weary. She felt nauseous and her breathing was raspy. She was crawling now, no longer able to walk, and dragging her knees on the coarse bark. A cry was building up in her chest and her eyes were welling up with tears but she had no energy for despair. So, those tears soon dried up.

The time had come, she said to herself. She remembered the wet cave. All those frozen winters and the howling storms, the darkness, the utter emptiness of life. She remembered the wondrous forest and the sad monster. The tree. She kissed the tree and lay down and closed her eyes. To rest.

Within moments, a light came on. If it was not the sun peeking through the foliage, then it would be the moon. She knew it and was pleased. She reached out and found a hand, now, two hands, more hands, a tiny hand, and she let hers be held in the most soft and steady embrace.

She awoke sometime later. She found herself in a large, comfortable bed under an extraordinarily colourful patchwork blanket. It was mostly quiet except for a whistling of a small wind and the rustling of leaves outside her window. Her hands, feet, and knees were bandaged up, loosely. On the bedside table next to her was a glass of water and a sweet-smelling pastry. Small, jaunty bricks with colourful letters, spelled out the words, Amar and Mama.

She thought about the monster. Those lost, tired eyes, the frail body only kept warm by a cloak of leaves, the pleading palms. She thought about the transformation and remembered how the crackling and braying had finally quietened.

Through the window, she looked out at the vast sky of blue azure. Her grandmother's book lay right next to her and she hugged it closely to her body. The memories of her grandmother were alive and vibrant in her mind. As were the memories of her small child, her mother and father, her sisters, her brothers.

She was alone. But she still had the songs and poetry and the stories and chants of her people. She now wanted to live, to speak them, and sing them. She had something to tell the world and she wanted to spend the rest of her life doing so.

On the other side of the room, behind a golden metallic grate, a small fire was crackling away. Propped up against the mantelpiece above the fire were several framed photographs. She recognised one of them and was overcome by the most powerful wave of love.

CHAPTER SIX

THE MAGIC CHIMNEY

By Samantha Pinazza

A cold winter night

The cart struggled in the snow, as the sun slowly fell to the horizon. Large white clouds thickened, promising another snowfall.

The exhausted horse shook his head, waving his mane to the right and left and bending his ears as if he wanted to shake off the approaching cold. When he snorted, his breath condensed into a cloud.

Already twice Ilya had to jump down from the cassette seat to free the heavy wheels that, sinking in the snow, could no longer advance. Finally, he had not gone up again, preferring to walk next to the cart: a little not to weigh further on that poor beast, a little to be faster in freeing the wheels.

The wind was blowing, icy as a witch's breath, lifting the boy's old coat, forced to walk with his hands tucked under his armpits to warm up a little. When, for a moment, the wind stopped blowing, Ilya was under the illusion to be safe, but suddenly it started again, more violent and merciless than before. It shouted and whistled, angry, rushing down from the snowy top of the mountains to descend with renewed violence on the plain, whipping with its volleys the poor cart.

The old father of Ilya, Boris, who held the reins cassette, sheltered as he could from those icy lashes sticking his neck in the gray wool scarf that he always put to go out: only the nose, completely red for the cold, came out of the rough fabric. The fur cap was well-worn on his bald head, often falling before his eyes.

They couldn't have gone on for long, with the icy air under their clothes. 'Father, it will be better to find accommodation for the night!' said Ilya, clapping a hand on the wagon bracket to draw the old man's attention.

'What? No, boy, no, we are still so far from Dravipol... in just three days there will be the market and you know we need that money.'

'Sure, but we might not get to Dravipol.' Ilya snorted, careful not to be heard. He didn't want to offend his father, displeasing him. He knew well how many sacrifices Boris had to face that winter: first the harvest of the summer was moldy, then the milk of the cows had begun to curdle. It almost seemed like their farm had been cursed.

Boris suspected Drusia, a woman who lived alone in the very back of the village, in a creaky old house where crows loved to rest between flights. She must have been a witch, and if there was one thing Boris just couldn't stand, it was magic. Ilya thought that they were all nonsense, he didn't believe in the supernatural and saw in Drusia only a grouchy shrew who preferred to be with her cats rather than with the other inhabitants of the village.

For Boris it was very serious that his son didn't believe in magic: in this way he put himself in danger, exposing to any possible deception. However, he had never been able to prove him wrong.

However, with all the misfortunes at the farm, Boris had no choice but to pick up some of the excellent cheeses he had prepared during the summer and his wife's best yarns to sell them at the big market in Dravipol. It was there, in fact, that the best deals were made: city people were willing to pay more for the excellent products of a farm and for the warm wool shawls of the countryside.

They had to arrive in time, however, otherwise they would not be able to sell even a slice of that good cheese. The competition would have been ruthless.

They went on for a while, Ilya and the horse with resigned air, the old man with a firm look. If he could load the wagon on his back and run to Dravipol, he would have done so immediately. Instead, without him noticing, the years had begun to weigh on his shoulders, once so strong and, by now, he couldn't even lift two buckets of milk alone.

Boris fixed his hands for a moment, fragile under the wool gloves: as old age progressed he was increasingly worried about his son, so careless, so skeptical. He'd end up in trouble.

A sudden snowflake carried by the wind landed on Boris's red nose, then another, a third... from the white clouds had started to fall a heavy snowfall. After a few minutes, the old man could no longer distinguish anything in front of him: he would certainly have lost his way. The path, in fact, was rapidly disappearing under that white blanket.

Ilya was unfortunately right, they had to stop, Boris thought reluctantly. And then, almost as if his thoughts had suddenly taken shape, on the side of the road he began to distinguish the warm and reassuring glare of lighted windows: it was an inn and, apparently, a beautiful fire burned inside.

The chimney

Father and son left the horse in the stable under the care of a plump, affable-looking boy and hurried into the inn. It was a very nice and cozy place, with a fire crackling in the fireplace and many ham from the appetizing air that hung from the ceiling behind the counter.

The hostess, a middle-aged woman with her hair gathered in a bun, made them sit in the common room, where many guests already sat at the wooden tables chatting and playing cards.

Boris felt much better now that he was no longer exposed to the icy gusts and could look at the snowfall at ease through the thick window glass, as he stretched his feet towards the crackling fire and drank a good cup of warm tea.

Ilya also felt happier: the hostess, Mrs Sofya, was very prompt and kind. In addition, she had brought him hot soup and some bread with roast meat to appease the hungry stomach. Nothing like a good meal for a boy. The father, however, had settled for the soup, and then began to yawn conspicuously.

The clock was only ten and a half, but the long journey had tired the young as much as the old.

'It's bedtime, my boy. We'll have to get up very early tomorrow to make up for lost time. Hopefully, in the meantime, it'll stop snowing.'

'Yes, Father.' Ilya had risen from the bench where he sat and had hurried to give a hand to the old man to climb the flight of stairs leading to the rooms. Madame Sofya made her way with a candle. Between the rooms and the common room there was only a loft, so the chatter of the patrons reached up there. Not that it was a problem: Boris, when he fell asleep, he wouldn't even feel an earthquake.

As soon as they arrived at one of the wooden doors, the woman opened it, left the candle to the guests and recommended: 'This is an old house, so every now and then groan and creak, but you needn't fear. Whatever noise you may hear, stay in bed and enjoy a good night's sleep.' Then she left with a smile.

Ilya thought that remark strange. What was the need to recommend staying in bed? He had laid down in the nice warm bed that was waiting for him trying not to think about it anymore, but no matter how he turned around between the covers, he couldn't get that suspicion out of his mind. His father, on the other hand, fell asleep as soon as his bald head touched the pillow.

Agitated, Ilya decided to stay awake, to see if there was anything really strange behind the words of the hostess or if, more likely, he was just imagining everything. Many times sleep tried to get better on him, so Ilya left the comfortable bed and listened by the door. When even the last guest had left the inn, silence fell everywhere.

It seemed that nothing would happen and the boy was about to go to sleep, resigned, when, around midnight, he heard the planks of the corridor creaking and hasty steps down the stairs. Trying to be as quiet as possible, he opened the door and snuck onto the landing, observing the common room that lay below him.

There, dressed as if she were going out, was Mrs Sofya, intent on stoking the fire of the fireplace so that it would not go out.

Ilya looked at her intrigued: the woman walked well over her fur cap and smoothed the folds of a long black cloak, looking at herself in a small round mirror hanging on the wall. The boy could not help but think that it was a bizarre outfit: a woolen coat would certainly be warmer than that fluttering cloak.

The woman, after settling her long hair, which she had freed from the bun to let it fall on the shoulders, had stretched her hand towards the mantel, grabbing a wooden box. She opened it with trepidation and extracted an ointment with which she began to rub her hands vigorously.

To Ilya that scene seemed increasingly bizarre. Suddenly, however, his thoughts were abruptly interrupted by a violent blow: it was the chimney, which growled almost its own life.

The noise grew louder and louder, when the strange wind blew the woman, lifting her from the ground and making her disappear through the hood, up the chimney. Ilya rubbed his eyes, incredulous: could the mistress have really disappeared?

The boy hurried down the stairs and approached the fireplace and looked up the hood: there was no trace of Mrs Sofya. Any chance she just disappeared?

Ilya was too curious to resist: he grabbed the wooden box and smelled its contents. The cream inside was gray as ash and had a pungent, annoying smell. He took some and began to rub his hands as he had seen the mistress do.

Immediately, the wind started to blow again, wrapping around his body. Ilya felt himself lifted from the ground and dragged up, higher and higher, along the narrow and dark tunnel of the chimney.

The ritual

Ilya felt a dull pain when he fell to the ground, rolling in the snow. He hurried up, dusting his clothes and massaging his sore shoulder.

How did he get there? He was in the woods and right in front of him there was a clearing with a frozen lake in the middle. He was amazed: could the magic chimney really have carried him there?

Rumors made him wince: if he was there, Mrs Sofya had to be there too and apparently she wasn't alone. Ilya felt it was wiser to hide, so he stooped, seeking shelter under the snow-covered branches of a large pine tree.

There were shadows moving by the frozen lake, but he couldn't understand what they were saying.

Suddenly, a fire broke out right in the middle of the lake. The incredible thing was that the ice didn't seem to melt, as if the fire was actually very cold. Thanks to that glow, the boy managed to distinguish the mistress and four other women. All of them wore a black cloak and their long hair down. Mrs Sofya got rid of the fur cap.

Then, a sudden explosion and out of nowhere a sixth woman appeared: Ilya opened his eyes, it was Drusia, the woman his father considered a witch! How did she appear out of nowhere? Did she also have a magic fireplace like the inn's?

The woman hurried toward her companions with their arms raised, ready to embrace them one by one. Ilya took the opportunity to get closer, always staying in the shelter of the trees.

'My dear, what a pleasure to see you again!' was saying an old woman leaning on her stick, the hooked nose that made her look like a crow. 'Now we can get started.'

The women approached the fire, starting to turn in circles: Mrs Sofya tore a lock of her hair and threw it into the fire, saying: 'this year I have made dozens of travelers go astray in the snow and I have transformed an irritating family into a beautiful set of dining chairs.'

'I,' went on a fat woman with ruddy cheeks, 'I turned my rivals into sows and imprisoned a handsome young man in a tree.' That said, she hurried to throw a black lock into the flames.

'I grew nightshade instead of wheat in the farmer's meadow and I changed all the grains in crawling insects' the old woman laughed, tearing a gray lock.

'My neighbor's hens have stopped making eggs, but his daughters have started laying them in their place.' A redheaded witch laughed, throwing her tribute into the fire.

'I bankrupted the obnoxious cloth merchant of my village,' exclaimed a small woman who almost disappeared under her cloak. 'One morning he woke up and found he could no longer touch his precious fabrics without turning them into cobwebs'. Another strand ended in fire.

'I made my neighbor's milk curdle,' continued Drusia, 'and I rotted all his harvest'. Ilya trembled with anger: so his father had always been right!

When the sixth strand of hair also ended in fire, the witches began to transform: their shadows, projected away from the bright light, seemed to stretch and deform until there were no more women before the incredulous eyes of the boy, but demons with blue bodies, long shaggy tails and hooves drumming on the icy surface. Their horns were frightening to behold, but even worse the beastly laughter that came out of those wicked throats.

Ilya, frightened, decided that it was time to escape: he had seen enough and would never again question his father's words. Now he was more than ever willing to believe in magic and stay away from it.

He started running into the woods, moving away from that scary bonfire. However, he had only taken a few steps that he felt slipping to the ground and fell violently. Something had grabbed him at the ankle: it was a long blue tail.

One of the demons had captured him and was leading him towards the others. The monsters were running, jumping the pony above the fire. The boy felt his heart pounding in his chest, terrified.

'Girls, we have company!' laughed the demon who had captured him, probably the short woman.

'What do we do about it? We kill it?' proposed the old witch.

'But I know him, this one, he's the son of the farmer to whom I ruined the harvest! How did he end up here?' Drusia was surprised.

'I know how! He snuck into my fireplace!' Said Mrs Sofya, 'he and his father are sleeping in my inn!'

'Please don't kill me!' begged Ilya, 'I won't say anything about what I saw.'

'Kill you? No, I don't think so,' replied the fat woman, even bigger as a demon than a witch. 'But we have to teach you a lesson: didn't anyone tell you that eavesdropping is not good?'

'And steal?' The mistress intervened.

Ilya had a beautiful oath and to avert: the witches, deaf to his supplications, threw him in the enchanted flames.

The boy felt a sudden chill and fainted from fear. When he woke up the next day, he found himself in the same room he had left the night before and Boris was waking up, rubbing his eyes.

'Father, father!' He screamed, glad to see him again. But nothing, not a sound came out of his mouth. He tried again, but still nothing. He tried to lift his hands to feel his throat, but couldn't move them. His body had become stiff as a piece of wood. The witches had turned it into an armchair.

Long the poor Boris sought his son, but in the end he had to leave without him. The memory of the boy was slowly fading from his mind and, by sunset, it would have disappeared altogether.

As for the boy, his destiny was to remain imprisoned in the form of an armchair, forever confined right in the room from which he had been advised not to leave. He would only grow old with his regrets, a prisoner of the magic he didn't want to believe in. This is what happened to spy on witches' secret rituals!

CHAPTER SEVEN

MR. JOHNSON'S FORMULAS

By Peter Collins

I don't know if you've ever been to hell. I visited once a fortnight; a ritual humiliation that took place every other Friday morning in an ordinary secondary school in a quiet suburb of South East London. In our school the lessons were spread over a two-week period. The teachers always referred to them as Red Week and Blue Week; as if they thought we kids were all too stupid to work out how many weeks there were in a fortnight. So this Friday morning in Blue Week an oh so familiar scene was being played out. There I was, standing in front of the class, haplessly trying to write out a chemical formula on the white board, while our Chemistry Teacher, Mr Johnson, stood behind me hurling insults as if they were confetti at a wedding. He was a heavy set man in his late forties, with untidy ginger hair and an ugly, puckered scar on his left cheek. He was in full flow.

'I said baking soda you idiot; sodium hydrogen carbonate. What have you put on the board?'

I looked up at the combination of letters and numbers I had written; NaClO H2O2. Na was definitely sodium. H was hydrogen. I thought I must be pretty close. Mr Johnson though obviously disagreed. His face had gone puce and there was spittle dripping from his lips. Not for the first time, I wondered just why he hated me so much.

'That's liquid sodium hypochlorite, you moron. I hope your mum doesn't use that in her baking; it's bleach! On the other hand, she might be doing the world a favour if she added it to your meals. There'd be one less idiot to pollute the gene pool.'

He put his head in his hands in dramatic mock despair. Or maybe it was real despair; I couldn't tell.

'One last chance to see if you've learned anything, boy. What sort of reaction do you get when you mix nitric acid and ethanol?'

I looked blankly at him for a moment until he threw his hands in the air.

'Exothermic, you idiot. Exo-bloody-thermic. Here!'

He reached back and picked up a heavy textbook from his desk and hurled it straight at me. I still had the marker pen and board rubber in my hands, so it was all I could do to raise my arms and stop it from crashing into my head. The book hit my elbow and fell heavily to the floor.

'Pick it up, boy!' There was a menacing tone to his words and the class went deathly still.

'Sit at your desk and look it up. Exothermic.'

He waited until I had found the correct page.

'Now try and learn something!' He paused for dramatic effect. I knew what was coming next. Everybody knew what was coming next. He said the same thing to me at the end of every lesson. It was a key part of Mr Johnson's ritual.

'It'll be a famous day when you get a formula right, boy. A famous day indeed. But I'm not holding my breath just yet. The day you get a formula right will be the day I die.'

As he walked away I got a few sympathetic looks from the rest of the class. I know it all sounds dramatic, but this was pretty much par for the course with Mr Johnson. It was ironic really. All of us kids were given assemblies about treating each other fairly, but the biggest bully in the school was a member of staff. He wasn't even a good teacher. He was well known for forgetting his experiments and he often had to come to the lab early to practise on his own before a lesson. I really had no idea why he took so much against me. There was no reason for it; he just detested me. Perhaps I should have been grateful for that. Imagine what he would have been like if he really did have a reason to hate me?

I briefly considered telling the Head of Year, but decided against it. They never listened when we complained about being bullied by another pupil. Imagine what it would be like complaining about a teacher? So I just let it be. There was no Chemistry in Red Week so I was safe from my ritual embarrassment for another fortnight.

Red Week actually started out really good for me. On Monday morning, Mrs Brown, our Form Teacher, took the register and then turned to us.

'Everybody, we have a new girl in the class, Jenny Patel. Jenny has switched to us from St Oswald's. Jenny, please step forward.'

Jenny moved next to her and stood there looking shyly at the class. She was small and dark and very pretty and I fell for her there and then. And, boy I fell hard, like a monkey down a well.

Mrs Brown was still talking. 'I know it's hard when you join a class part way through term, Jenny, but our school has a buddy system for new starters.' She indicated me with an imperious wave of her hand. Teachers always thought they could get you to do something just by clicking their fingers. It normally irritated me, but today I was in no mood to object.

'Josh here will be your buddy. He'll show you around the school and look after you. Is that OK?'

She nodded shyly as Mrs Brown pointed to the desk next to mine. For the whole week, she was always by my side. She was as nice as she was pretty and, believe it or not, she liked me too. I kept telling everybody I was only spending time with her because of the buddy system, but I don't think anybody bought it.

But my heart sank when the Friday of Blue Week came around again. I was sure Mr Johnson was going to target me and I didn't want to be humiliated in front of Jenny. It was all I could think about on the way to the lab. It was a pain going to the science lab. It was an old portacabin near the playing fields. It was always cold because the windows didn't shut properly. The school was always promising to build a new lab in the main building, but it never happened.

As it turned out, I was as wrong as I'd ever been. Mr Johnson stood at the front of the class like an actor taking centre stage. He couldn't contain his glee.

'Ah, we have a celebrity in class, everybody. Miss Patel, step to the front, please.'

Jenny walked nervously to the board. Mr Johnson fixed her with a tight, unpleasant smile.

'Councillor Patel made local air pollution a large part of his election platform, didn't he? Perhaps you'll explain to the class the various elements of smog.'

Jenny hesitated for a moment and then said, 'Sir, smog is caused by car fumes mixing with fog.'

Mr Johnson's voice was suddenly a shout. 'I know that, you idiot. I asked for the chemical formula.'

'Er, we didn't do that at my last school, sir.'

Mr Johnson smacked his hand so hard on the desk that a cloud of dust rose in the air. We were well used to his outbursts, but he seemed even more strained today. The whole class seemed to sense the tension.

'I didn't ask for a lecture on how the school syllabus is applied, Patel.' Mr Johnson was almost shaking with rage. 'I'm talking about Volatile Organic Compounds and tropospheric ozone. Write out the formula for peroxyacetyl nitrate now!'

'I don't know it, sir.' Jenny was in tears by now.

'Don't know it? Don't know it? I thought Councillor Patel knew everything.'

Mr Johnson was shouting so loudly, the PE teacher who was organising a volleyball game on the playing field outside put her head round the door wearing a quizzical expression. Seeing her, Mr Johnson pulled himself together. He put a hand up to her and faced the class.

'Right. Patel, see me afterwards for detention. Everybody else turn to page 73 of your book.'

Next lesson I had French, and Jenny had German so we didn't speak until lunchtime. Mr Johnson had given her an hour's detention after school.

'Why's he so mad at you?' I asked.

She sighed. 'It's the Councillor thing. Mr Johnson stood as a candidate for some right wing party at the local council. He kept saying immigrants should go home. My dad stood as an independent and beat him. So he hates my dad twice over. First for being Indian and second for beating him. It looks like he's going to take it out on me.'

I tried to process it all. I knew what Mr Johnson was like with me for no reason. I could only imagine how he might treat Jenny if he felt he had a real grievance.

'Can you get your dad to do something?'

'No. I don't want to upset him.' She took my hand and turned those beautiful brown eyes on me. 'But you'll help me through it, won't you Josh?'

I nodded and squeezed her hand tightly. But then we let go quickly before anybody started taking the mick. Schools are like that.

That afternoon I nearly gave Mrs Brown a heart attack by staying late in the library to do my homework. But it meant I was there for Jenny when she came out of detention. Straight away I could see she was upset.

'What's the matter?'

'He was horrible.'

I bit my lip, not wanting to rush her.

'Go on.'

'He kept calling me names. I mean really nasty horrible things. And then he kept standing right by me. He put his hands on my neck.'

She shuddered.

'Did he hurt you?'

'No. Well not really. But it was like he was showing me he could hurt me any time he wanted.'

'Well, let's go and see Mrs Brown.'

'No. We can't. I mean it's just my word against his. He's been here forever. He'll say I'm just a new girl causing trouble.'

She started to cry and I held her tightly wondering how on earth I could help her.

For the next six weeks it gradually got worse. It seemed that Mr Johnson had passed on all his anger towards Jenny; and passed it on with a vengeance. Every other Friday morning, Mr Johnson would taunt Jenny in front of the class for the whole two hours, and put her in detention for the slightest thing. In the detentions with nobody else around, his treatment of her got more and more unpleasant. I tried to provoke him so he'd get angry with me instead, but he'd lost interest in me completely.

As we walked home on the Thursday of another Blue Week I could see that Jenny was at the end of her tether. She looked drawn and tired and she seemed afraid of everything.

'I'm scared, Josh.'

I started to say something, but she rushed on.

'No. I mean I'm really scared. Last week in detention, he said he was setting up an experiment for Friday's lesson, using nitric acid. And if I got anything wrong then it'd be detention again. And this time...'

She hesitated as if she couldn't get the words out. 'This time I'd really get what was coming to me.'

I tried to tell her it would be all right, but we both knew they were just empty words. When I got home, I racked my brains to think of something I could do. I desperately wanted to switch places with Jenny, but I knew that was impossible. In the end, all I could manage was to pray for a miracle. I slept badly that night and was still wide awake at the crack of dawn.

I was almost shaking with nerves in Mrs Brown's class assembly that morning. She was going on about road safety or something, but I could barely concentrate. She was just handing out some leaflets when we heard a muffled thud from outside, rather like a loud car backfire. After a few moments, one of the teaching assistants came in and whispered something to Mrs Brown. Mrs Brown immediately left telling the rest of us to wait in the classroom. We could hear sirens and a lot of commotion while we waited. There was a lot of gossip and speculation and it was half an hour before Mrs Brown came back in with a serious look on her face.

'Class, I am afraid there has been a tragic accident in the science lab. I'm very sorry to announce that Mr Johnson is dead.'

My nerves overcame me and I almost passed out. It emerged that Mr Johnson had arrived at the lab early to do some preparatory work for our lesson and there had been some sort of mix up with the chemicals he had used which had led to a fatal explosion. Everybody was pretty shocked. Nobody had really liked him but only Jenny and I knew anything about the real Mr Johnson. It seemed that I had got my miracle after all. I tried to comfort Jenny by telling her that although it was a terrible accident, at least this would stop him hurting more innocent people in the future. We had a school assembly later in the week where everybody was warned about the dangers of lab experiments. And the school got a terrible report about inadequate safety measures and the dilapidated state of the lab. There was a memorial service for Mr Johnson the following week. And then a new lab was hastily built in the main building, a new teacher was appointed and life moved on.

We sat our exams later that year. I got a B in Chemistry. It turned out I did know some formulas after all. The new teacher was pretty good, but I can't give her all the credit. Mr Johnson had taught me a few things. For instance, I knew that exothermic meant the release of heat; in other words an explosion. I wasn't going to forget that after he told me how dangerous it was to mix nitric acid and ethanol. Because I'd been so worried about Jenny I'd been wide awake at dawn on that Friday morning and it hadn't been too difficult to get to the lab early. Being an outbuilding, it wasn't covered by the burglar alarm, and the faulty window locks meant that it was no problem to get in. Once in, all I had to do was switch a few labels on some of the storage jars. That was all really. I couldn't switch places with Jenny, but I could switch a few labels. I knew that Mr Johnson was always a bit shaky about his experiments and I'd gambled that he would turn up early on his own to rehearse them like he normally did. It turned out I was right.

I know it sounds awful, but I had no regrets at all about what I'd done. Mr Johnson had been a horrible and unpleasant man who had been on the verge of doing something terrible to Jenny. If I hadn't switched the chemicals, heaven knows what he would have done. He deserved everything he got. He hadn't even been a good teacher; his lesson was just ritual bullying. But I had to give him credit for one thing. The ending to his ritual always contained one very accurate prediction. The day I got a formula right was the day he died.

CHAPTER EIGHT

AN UPROOTED PRESENCE

By Vaibhav Pradeep Gilankar

This was the most appropriate time to perform any ritual from the pages of "Rogue Songs of Olden Times".

Outside the house, tall trees were standing all around. Their branches, covered by the hanging bats, looked like saggy arms spread by weak old men. The full moon trying hard to shove its light through the entirely clouded sky seemed like a faint blood stain that makes itself visible from beneath the bandage put on a nasty scar.

On such a night, I was witnessing a horrible thing that I had never expected to see in this house.

"We summon you! We summon you!", as the chanting grew more rapid, Mr. Mhatre tightened his grip on his double-edged sword and raised it in the air. From the barn, Sholia, my most favorite buck, was brought for the sacrifice. Neither him nor Pawan, his son, seemed like they were feeling sad to kill that poor animal and what could I do but watch? Afterall, I wasn't a part of this family. At the moment when Mr. Mhatre was about to cut off Sholia's head, I closed my eyes, bit my lips and quickly grabbed Mrs. Mhatre's hand who was standing beside me.

"STOP!", Pawan suddenly cried, "Fa... fa.. father, look!"

I could not understand why Pawan was pointing at me. Mr. Mhatre was surely shocked enough to keep his mouth open wide and drop the sword...

This ritual was set into motion a month ago...

Mr. Mhatre and his family had always taken care of me. At first, they used to let me stay in their house but after some time they sent me to their barn to live. Normally, a girl would have taken this as an insult but quite frankly, I felt a lot more pleasure living in the barn than I ever did in the house. In the barn, I had befriended all the cows, goats, and their calves and lambs who would lick my hand, and make me smile. Among those, I loved Sholia more than anyone. He was a pearl white buck with two little horns over his head. His bleats provided a sweet soul to the warm, golden sun rays entering through the cracks of the barn roof in the morning. The way Sholia made me feel in the barn, I never felt that way when I used to live in the house, maybe because Mr. Mhatre and Pawan had managed to encompass the entire house in the cold shroud of their ambition. Their discussions would last till the late hours of the night and all of them would be centered only around "Rogue Songs of Olden Times", an ancient scripture passed down to Mr. Mhatre by his ancestors.

Pawan was studying the scripture thoroughly as per Mr. Mhatre's instructions. They were trying to perform a ritual for summoning a dead spirit from it. Pawan had a good understanding of its language therefore he was to read it and Mr. Mhatre was going to make sure that they had everything they needed for the ritual. Since last week they had been working excessively to prepare for it. In the night, they would come into the barn and go over it repeatedly, their murmuring had the same threatening vibrations as a cobra's hissing. I could listen to their conversations whenever they would come into the barn and last week, I heard Pawan say,

"Father, I've read the ritual carefully and it needs only five things."

"What are they?"

"First, a dozen green twigs of sable licorice, which I will bring from the forest. Second, the most loved piece of cloth or belonging of the dead that we wish to invoke. Third, a knife whetted on the skull of a widow or a widower. Fourth, a marble statue of Meena Somkanti, which I didn't understand-"

"We have it, we have her marble statue, don't worry, just continue."

"And um... the fifth thing is... uh..."

"What's the fifth thing?! Speak already!"

"A blue hawk...", Pawan sighed, "I'm... I'm sorry father but I don't think it'll be possible to get it."

"What?!", Mr. Mhatre gnashed his teeth, he grabbed Pawan's head and brought his face closer to speak in lower tone,

"Say that again and I'll break your jaw."

"Fa... father, please!", Pawan was scared, "Listen, father, blue hawks are the rarest of bird species in the whole world and to get one is almost-"

"SHUT UP!", this time Mr. Mhatre didn't even bother to whisper and slapped Pawan hard, "Whatever the ritual needs, we will provide it!"

"But father, to get our hands on a blue hawk will cost us both an indefinite period of time and an unimaginable amount of money which we can't afford!"

"Do you think I'm a fool!?", Mr. Mhatre scoffed, "I've already got a blue hawk in my sights and it's not even far away."

"A blue hawk? Here in our city!?", Pawan shrieked in disbelief.

"Yes, and we will get it tomorrow, by whatever cost it takes!", Mr. Mhatre stomped his foot and then they both left the barn.

A few moments later, Mrs. Mhatre came to me,

"They were both talking about the ritual, weren't they?", her voice was sweating with sorrow.

"Yes", I politely answered, "They were talking about getting a blue hawk tomorrow. Oh, wouldn't it be nice, Mrs. Mhatre? To have a little bird in our house..."

"Our?"

"Oh... I... I meant in your... your house..."

"Don't apologize, dear", she caressed me, "I've always considered you to be a part of this family but they haven't, that's why they've put you here in this barn like some old relic. I tried telling them both to keep you in the house but they never listen to me."

"But I like it here, Mrs. Mhatre!"

"Of course, you do, dear", Mrs. Mhatre smiled, "I wish I could also make myself happy at anyplace like you do. But my husband and my son are disturbing my peace. I've been trying to tell them to just cease the thought of performing that useless, ridiculous ritual, it won't do anything but-"

"But they never listen to you."

"Right", she sighed, "I guess the only thing we can do is watch…"

Mrs. Mhatre left and I kept thinking about what Mr. Mhatre and Pawan were talking… A blue hawk? Where would they get a blue hawk?

Next morning, while I was playing with Sholia in the barn, I saw an old man coming with Mr. Mhatre and Pawan to the house. The old man must have been ten to twelve years older than Mr. Mhatre, he was dressed well and holding something in his hand covered with white cloth over it. They all were talking in a friendly manner.

"And this is my house, Dr. Prabhakar!", Mr. Mhatre said to the old man, like showing him an exhibit from a museum.

"Ahh, so lovely!", Dr. Prabhakar fixed his glasses and admired the house, "Right in the arms of nature you've built it! Is that your barn? You wouldn't mind me taking a look inside, would you?"

"Uh… no, I mean yes, that's our barn… but perhaps, first you'd like to have some tea in the house-", Pawan was opposing the doctor from going into the barn but-

"Nonsense Pawan!", Mr. Mhatre slapped the back of his head, "If Dr. Prabhakar wants to take a look inside the barn, then he shall! Let's go, doctor."

Dr. Prabhakar entered the barn with Mr. Mhatre and Pawan. He was looking around at the cows and goats and he even petted some of them.

"Ah ha! These animals are so fine! Wonders of nature itself!", the doctor sounded funny while covering his nose with a handkerchief.

"Dr. Prabhakar…", Mr. Mhatre said, "I must tell you the reason for inviting you here…"

"Oh of course, I already know that!", the doctor smirked and he removed the white cloth from the cage that was in

his hand. Inside the cage was kept a magnificent avian that I had never seen before!

It had feathers of sky-blue hue, with totally black eyes and talons so sharp that they could have pierced any hide.

"No, doctor, you don't know...", Mr. Mhatre's voice turned grim, "We've called you here today because we want that bird."

"What?!", Dr. Prabhakar recoiled from Mr. Mhatre in surprise, "But... but you told to me that-"

"Ye... yes, doctor", Pawan stuttered, "I'm sorry we lied to you. But don't worry, we can pay you handsomely like... uh... like this barn for instance! Each and every one of these fine animals you see here will be yours if you just-"

"Are you out of your mind?!", Dr. Prabhakar frowned and burst in anger, "These stinking cows and goats for this... this extraordinary and exquisite rare blue hawk?! Well, excuse me but I shall leave now...", the doctor pushed Mr. Mhatre aside and started walking towards the barn door.

"Dr. Prabhakar, please!", Pawan rushed after him and pleaded, "We're... we're sorry but please try to underst-"

"SLASH!"

Mr. Mhatre swung his sword and a gush of blood splattered everywhere. Dr. Prabhakar's chopped off head dropped on the ground with a "THUMP!" and the blue hawk screeched as its cage fell from the doctor's hand.

"Fa... father.... What did you do?", Pawan backed away from Dr. Prabhakar's body and pulled his own hair anxiously, "Where... where did you get that sword?"

"This old thing?", Mr. Mhatre calmly cleaned the blade with his own shirt, "I had hidden it right here in this haystack. Now, take that bird inside."

"But... but father, what about the doctor's corpse? You've decapitated him-"

"Calm down, we'll need his head. We require the skull of a widow or a widower to whet the knife, remember? And I would've killed him for the blue hawk anyway, Pawan! You've read the "Rogue Songs...", right? You must have noticed how all the darkest rituals for summoning the dead require a blue hawk sacrifice, but did you understand why?"

"No..."

"Our ancestors have passed on this knowledge, my son. Death always sends her silent shrieks into the living world and the echoes of those shrieks bring all those souls who have completed their mortal time back to her. But then our ancestors discovered something remarkable! They realized that the blue hawks possess their own, separate death shrieks. Meaning, wherever we kill an enchanted blue hawk, its death will shriek silently from that place then its echo will bring back and bind the soul we wish to summon through the ritual! The only thing the ritual requires is for that dead blue hawk to be hung by the neck of a sacrificial animal like a goat or a cow or-"

"But why only the blue hawks?", Pawan asked in confusion.

"No one knows, but what matters now is that we have got one and-", Mr. Mhatre's sight suddenly fell on me and he stopped talking.

"What happened, father?", Pawan asked.

"Nothing, bring a buck or a goat from this herd for the ritual", Mr. Mhatre fixed his horrifying blue eyes on me. With his wrinkled, scrawny finger pointed at me, he told Pawan, "And bring her too into the house..."

***

Tonight, Mr. Mhatre and Pawan had gathered everything required for the ritual in the main hall of the house.

THE SELECTION OF A SACRED STRAWBERRY

"The knife whetted on Dr. Prabhakar's skull?" Mr. Mhatre was reading the list.

"Got it", Pawan confirmed.

"A dozen green twigs of the sable licorice?"

"Check,"

"A sacrificial animal... Oh you brought Sholia, huh?"

"Yes, he's a fine buck, right?", Pawan caressed the back of poor Sholia, I was resisting my tears seeing him like that, completely unaware about what was to happen with him.

"Yes, he is. Next thing, a piece of cloth loved by the spirit we wish to-"

"I've brought the pink gown..."

"And the marble statue of Meena Somkanti? Oh, yes, it's right there. So, we've got everything. Let's begin."

"Yes, father", Pawan said. First, he made a circle with the twigs of sable licorice and brought Sholia into the circle.

"Bring me the whetted knife...", Mr. Mhatre said to Pawan and from the cage, took out the blue hawk, which began to flap its wings and screech, but Mr. Mhatre's grip on its legs was tight.

The knife blade shined for a second when Mr. Mhatre took it from Pawan's hand. He stepped into the circle and just like that, brutally slit the blue hawk with that knife, he let its blood flow down on Sholia and in the whole area inside the licorice circle. The helpless hawk twitched while the death was gouging its life out and soon turned cold. Pawan wound a string around it and hung it by Sholia's neck. I couldn't believe that Sholia, a fair, sweet looking buck had now become hideous with a dead bird around his neck and blood all over his body.

"We summon you, our beloved! We summon you!", Mr. Mhatre took the same sword with which he had decapitated Dr. Prabhakar and began to chant loudly. Pawan put the pink gown over Sholia's back and stood outside the circle to watch what happened.

As the chanting grew louder and rapid, Mr. Mhatre raised the sword in the air. Just when he was about to bring it down with all his might, I closed my eyes, bit my lips and grabbed Mrs. Mhatre's hand tightly.

"STOP!", Pawan cried, "Fa... father... lo... look!"

As a loud "clunk" echoed in the hall, I opened my eyes and saw Mr. Mhatre had dropped the sword. His mouth was opened wide, both he and Pawan were looking at Mrs. Mhatre in shock. Their hair turned white due to fear.

"What happened, dear husband?", the translucent, pale white figure of Mrs. Mhatre asked Mr. Mhatre, "Even when I was alive, I used to tell you that none of those rituals can do what they claim."

"You... But how... how can you be-", Mr. Mhatre's words were crumbling under his disbelief.

"How can I be here?", Mrs. Mhatre sighed, "I was always present, dear husband. No ritual was needed to call or 'bind' me here."

"M... Mother...", Pawan shuddered, "How... how is that possible?", he pointed at my hand holding Mrs. Mhatre's.

"Oh, my sweet Pawan, even I have been unable to understand her...", Mr. Mhatre smiled at me and caressed my marble hand, "But I know for sure that Meena here has been the only one who could see me and listen to me and I was also the only one who could talk to her, maybe because she's more human than you both could ever be... That's why even though being made of dense, cold marble, she demonstrated the warmth of her compassion tonight by holding my hand and averting herself from seeing your monstrosity. I would've stayed if you had desired my love, but you still wish to control me even after my demise and that's enough for me to uproot my presence from this place."

A cold breeze entered the hall and with it, Mrs. Mhatre's pale spirit effaced but not before kissing me on my cheek and saying,

"Take care, dear Meena Somkant!... Farewell."

Mr. Mhatre and Pawan fell on their knees and wept for losing Mrs. Mhatre for the last time. I kept watching them as I always have.

CHAPTER NINE

True Love

By Philip Stenström

His face was firm, weathered and hardened by time and elements. He had a devilish appearance, he was muscular and strong, but also kind. He was big and tall with hands full of scars. His hair was oat-colored and golden like sunshine. He stood in the yard in his blue collared clothes and thick boots. The spring wind played in his hair and caressed his cheek. The sun glistened in the beads of sweat on his forehead. With a face stiff with shame and tenderness, he saw Alma driving away along the country road with the pickup. He drew a long sigh when it disappeared behind the trees. In a nearby pasture, a sheep was bleating and breaking the silence in the yard.

He had promised her that it wouldn't happen again. The promise was as broken as his soul and the bridge of trust between them was burnt down.

He had been completely sincere in his appeals and he had made an effort to straighten himself out so that Alma would calm down, but once again he had crossed the line. And now it felt as if love was eating him up from within.

Life was not worth a breath without Alma. He needed her as much as a cow needs grass under its hooves and mule. It was true love, even though he needed her love as much as he needed to vent his anger. Besides Alma, anger also seemed to be the only thing that made him feel alive.

As he stood there, he began to smell dried blood on his flannel shirt. His head, cheek and right eye throbbed with pain. He spat a jet of blood from the corner of his mouth with a grin of pain on his lips. A strong odor of shame, sweat and alcohol stood over him. He could never let go of the bottle when spring came, nor could he control his mood. It was like a curse that went down in the family, an inherited sin, embedded in his genes. He was convinced that he was Cain-marked. The built-up anger he had been wearing through-out the winter was always released during the spring like a bad ritual. He was strapped to the pole of shame that morning; everything was in a disgraceful mess. The sky, on the other hand, was clear and cleansed; innocent. Slowly, the spring sun dried up the dew.

With his head lowered, ashamed, he entered the old chalk-colored house. Carefully, he went into the kitchen. Cigarette butts and broken glass were scattered on the floor. The tumult and beatings still resounded in his fragile memory. He imagined how his hands became fists and how his chin stood straight out in anger. He shook off his memory, licked his dry lips and looked at the bottle of moonshine on the table. He stepped into the glass with his boots and sat down moaning on a worn kitchen chair that creaked under his weight. He cleared his throat and poured some of his moonshine into an unwashed, cloudy glass. His hand was furrowed and he noticed blows when he drank. He cared for his sore knuckle on his right hand and tried to imagine how he had beaten Bengt or if it had only been a dream. It burned in my throat before the alcohol finally settled in my stomach. He sipped again and closed his mouth again, which became a line. He stared into the fading wallpaper, unsure if he should laugh or cry, at last he lowered his gaze to the glass. Alma deserved someone better and an end to all these problems he had caused her.

In the room next door he heard someone stumble and a bang was heard in the desolate house. "Dammit all to hell," swore a raucous voice. Then a careless man stepped into the kitchen with crumpled clothes and a tattered hairstyle.

"What the hell are you doing, Karl?" shouted Robert. "You're worse than an elephant in a china shop."

"Who the hell pissed in your coffee?" Karl cut back with a sharp tongue and walked on unsafe legs to a kitchen chair and sat down. His face was stiff, his legs stiff and his hands as red as a boiled crayfish. Karl leaned forward and Robert felt his warm breath, felt his vapors and strong tobacco smell. Robert poured a glass on the table for his friend as a gift of reconciliation. Karl slapped his narcissistic lips, frowned, sipped it and stared at him, unsure if he should laugh or swear. "Really good stuff this!" he said with a grin of schadenfreude.

The silence subsided for a while and none of them said a single word, and even though they were hungover, they were used to it. It was their spring ritual.

A Black-and-Red-bug crawled across the table among glasses, cigarette butts and empty beer cans. Karl caught it and mashed it between his claw-like fingers. Then he pursed the lips of the strong stench of the insect, which was its last stinking farewell to life.

Robert sipped his glass and glanced around the kitchen. "What the hell happened yesterday?"

"Don't you remember?" said Karl, wiping his hand clean on his worn-out jeans.

Robert shook his head.

"You made Bengt into minced meat yesterday", said Karl and laughed, he knew that Bengt deserved it but it did not stop him from thinking it was a violent and bloody experience.

Robert, whose skull had been cloudy during the morning, had had difficulty memorizing his memory, but gradually everything began to fall apart. "I warned him several times to shut his mouth," Robert said, sighing and realizing that the commotion the night before had not been a dream. He began to remember the incident in the kitchen as a nightmare, foggy and with lots of trouble and blood.

He remembered how his face turned red, how he tensed so that his hands shook, how his muscles developed and throbbed. The first blow, when he exploded with rage, everything flashed and vibrated within him. His eyes were flushed and wild with the glow of the lamplight and the moonshine. He saw himself flying at Bengt and burying his fist in his face. All the air blew out of him and he fell to the floor like a felled tree and landed on the floor with a muffled sound.

He shook off the awful image of himself.

Karl fumbled for a pack of cigarettes and lit a cigarette. Robert blocked a cigarette to calm his nerves. He blew out the smoke against a window that stood on a gable and collapsed, as if he was relieved that he was not ignited by the alcohol vapors.

Everything in the kitchen smelled strong and disgusting.

Karl ashed in a crumpled empty jar on the table.

Robert sucked on his dried lower lip between his teeth and looked around. "How was Bengt?"

Karl grinned with a grin. "Damn, Robert, you ran over Bengt like a steamroller. He looked like a run over hedgehog when you were done with him ", he said and laughed." You go completely crazy, like a bull, when you're angry and get booze in you."

Robert sighed and caressed his sore knuckle.

Karl waved his hand as if the whole incident was trivial. "Bengt will recover, you don't have to feel bad for him."

Robert looked up in surprise with a bold smile. "Who said I felt bad for him?"

The following night the whole house was as dead and quiet as in a cemetery. Robert had tried to fall asleep that night, but he lay for a long time in the uncomfortable, lonely bed, staring up at the ceiling. Everything in the house was lonely and desolate. He missed Alma's body heat and lovely scent in the bed next door. Then a creeping feeling began to gnaw at him and kept him awake.

It had brightened a little outside when he realized that he heard footsteps in the gravel path outside. Robert got an eerie feeling again but then thought hopefully that it might be Alma. For a brief moment, a shining hope welled up in him at the thought that Alma had returned home.

He got up eagerly, the cold floorboards crackled and creaked like ice under his feet. He peeked out of the unwashed window in the dark but did not see a soul out there. The moon is still loose like a gloomy skull in the night sky.

Disappointed, he went into the bathroom, rinsed himself in the sink, and wiped himself thoroughly with a solidified bloody towel when he heard the creaking loudly downstairs. It was as if the whole house lived a life of its own; every creaking sound in the house sounded like a rocking ship on the high seas.

He hesitated, then slowly went down the creaking stairs. Found a cigarette in his shirt pocket and lit it. His eyes adjusted in the dark. His face suddenly became expressionless and gravely serious. In the dim light at the kitchen table he saw Bengt sitting with a shotgun in his arms.

Robert's face tightened, his fingers shook as he pulled a puff from the cigarette. The tip of the cigarette glowed as red as a brake light. Slowly he went to the table and sat down opposite Bengt.

Robert tried to both read his intentions and figure out what he was going to do next. Bengt patterned him, as if thinking about where he would best shoot and hit to cause the least blood splatter.

"Have you thought this through?" Robert asked in a visionary tone. Bengt stared at him and got every breath Robert took to wonder if that was the last thing he breathed.

Bengt's face was dark with boiling anger, if eyes could kill it was well close. He sat still, waiting with a rock-hard and unpleasant look. His eyes were black and empty, like small graves, and Robert began to shake a little in fear, but even though he saw that Bengt looked angry and impatient, he could not help but provoke him. The loneliness caused him to get into trouble sooner than usual.

"If you want an excuse, you can forget it," said Robert, Bengt called and grinned contentedly to build courage and defy fear. He sat quietly, steadfast and paralyzed. The house was completely quiet, it felt like he was locked in a coffin. The silence scared Robert the most. Bengt's face was swollen with bruises and insomnia; a raw and horrible picture. He was fraught with hatred and an aching desire to hurt Robert.

"I want you to go down on your knees and pray and ask for your life," Bengt finally said in an indifferent tone.

Robert valued his life highly, but he did not intend to devalue himself by kneeling and praying and praying for mercy, least of all for him. Bengt seemed to swell with anger and impatience, which led Robert to reconsider his strategy to a more diplomatic one. He blew a cloud of smoke against the ceiling. "Uh, come on," Robert said, "have a glass. You look like you need one."

Bengt glanced at one of the cloudy glasses on the messy table, frowned, pressed a finger to one of his nostrils and blew strings across the table. "I do not want to drink your piss," he replied angrily to the gift of atonement. "I said I want to see you on your knees."

A prolonged and tense silence arose again.

Outside, a car was suddenly heard driving into the courtyard and stole Bengt's attention. The next moment, Robert spread the cigarette against Bengt's face so that the embers cracked and flickered. Without thinking, Robert overturned the table in front of him so that the bottle and glasses shattered against the floor in a crashing sound.

Bengt, who had completely lost his temper, fumbled with the shotgun and dropped it on the floor and the noise filled the whole house.

Neck over head, Robert plunged out the front door in the direction of the dazzling headlights from the car in the yard.

Outside it was otherwise empty and quiet. The moon had a spooky halo over it in the daybreak. He cast a quick and wild, red-burst look behind him and saw Bengt coming rushing out of the house with the shotgun. He quickly applied and pressed off. Robert crouched just as the shot fired with a roaring explosion and heard the bullet vein pass over his head. He looked up with relief for a brief second before hearing a crashing sound that made his hair stand on end. He turned his head, and to your great sorrow he discovered Alma. She was staggering next to the car. "Oh, Robert," she said in a crisp, shaky voice before she, like a sack of potatoes, collapsed with a dull thud on the grass

He protectively reached Alma and went down on his knees in the dewy grass.

The skin on her face was smooth and relaxed. She smelled faintly of soap, as if she had just showered. She was wearing a white blouse and worn jeans, her medium length hair was loose. A large pool of blood was marked on her breast like a dark butterfly and it shone in the clear moonlight. Robert carefully corrected the chestnut fringe on her so he could see her face. Her face was colorless and empty, foreign and distant, as if she were slowly falling into a stunning eternal slumber. Her hands and skin were icy cold when he touched them.

"Robert," she whispered. Her eyes became glossy and closed after a while.

"Darling." He held her hand and tried to keep her alive and prayed that her breathing would not stop. When he looked at her, innocently lying on the damp ground, he suddenly felt a great sorrow well up inside him. There they were, husband and wife, one innocent, the other guilty of transgressions.

In the corner of his eye, a shadowy figure rushed past him with his breath in his throat and disappeared into the darkness. It was Bengt who hurried on with his face turned away, but Robert did not stop him, did not even think about the thought. Instead, Robert gently placed his head against Alma's chest, listening to her heart pounding until it stopped beating completely.

"Honey," he begged with a pleading tone and glossy eyes. "Came back!" He heard himself crying horse and meaningless, paralyzed by emptiness and despair. But no matter how much he begged and prayed, her voice never returned to him. He whispered her name, but it was pointless. She was gone, forever.

It became eerily quiet. In addition to a hedgehog rustling in a bush nearby, the yard was suddenly quiet again.

With a spooky, tear-filled and pale face, Robert looked up and watched a silver-gray fog slowly rising from the forest and sweeping over the newly plowed soil. As he sat there, a shy dawn rose behind the forest and Robert, filled with sorrow and remorse, watched the sunlight chase away the shadows like a bloodhound. And all the shame and fear he had carried was replaced by a huge loss.

CHAPTER TEN

THE RITUAL

By Lee Fountain

Each day, for the last three months, since her passing, I have made the same lonely pilgrimage to her grave-and each day I have been struck by the unending sadness that I had presumed the passage of time would erode into something more bearable, not less so. I suppose I could feel more at ease if I could somehow shake the sensation that she could still somehow be so terribly lonely out there, that Death was indeed final and for all of its other indignities and trespasses, did not somehow allow us to realise that we were dead-and so terribly alone.

So I come every day to talk to her. My preparations, the journey itself, even the chat, all have become something akin to a ritual that I feel will help rid her of loneliness-or me of the sense that by not going every day, I will be betraying her and condemning her to an eternal oblivion worse than that of her own unjust and untimely demise. Ironically, she passed on the first day of spring, though daffodils and crocuses that had already been fighting for early life before that day, were soon choked back out of existence first by a late and particularly cruel frost and then by heavy rainfall-the kind of deluge that lasts for days and makes you question if it will ever stop. Like her family's grief, it came in torrents and seemed that nothing could abate it, the ground around her grave becoming ever unstable and so waterlogged that I feared the very earth might burp her out of its watery bowels and she would then flow back out of the woods, down the ravine and would be lost to the ravenous ocean, foaming at the mouth atop the shards and boulders beyond the gulley and salt plains. What started as justifiable concern to be expected from the grieving became an obsession; a vigil to protect her within her fragile resting place and this in turn became my daily trek until He allowed my waking self to alight on the obvious solution for us both to end this loneliness and torturous misery. By this time, summer had sort of begun and on some days, I had even worked myself to something approaching a sweat by the time I reached her spot.

Some days, I walked in silence; others were spent in prayer that was more often than not said aloud as few, if any, ramblers came by this path given its steepness, exposure to the elements and sheer isolation. Those few that did seek the challenge of a more robust walk rarely made it all the way up into the woods beyond, for the cliffs grew ever more precipitous and one wrong foot combined with a particularly strong gust could prove fatal, so none but me came to her lonely graveyard and I simultaneously liked and disliked this fact. On one hand, it meant I had my peace and solace; on the other it heightened my perception of her solitude and abandonment and caused me much consternation and many sleepless nights, until the solution arrived.

THE SELECTION OF A SACRED STRAWBERRY

On one such sleepless night, in my hut less than three miles from where she lay (but still, a good three hours expedition in good conditions, even to someone as experienced with route, perils and location as me), I awoke from a particularly bad nightmare to see that a choking, freezing sea mist had stolen the stars and moonlight. Flashes of the dream grabbed at me through the fog within: mere remnants of the dream, soon to be lost like moths in the wind, leaving just traces of memories that would tickle like broken gossamer. A bloody hand. A bruised face. Broken eyes. Tendrils of tree roots like severed nerves reaching for something in the same darkness that blackened hands groped through in vain, desperately trying to grasp disembodied flesh. And a repeated phrase, but all that my waking brain would allow me to retrieve and retain was a solitary "Don't..."

I am deep in my preparations now for the solution that seems the only way to end both of our suffering and it is so logical (if not strictly rational) that I cannot believe I needed to trouble Him to help me find it. It was the day after the worst of the dreams and the sea-mist had thinned but was still hanging desperately on to my surroundings, lending everything a dankness and muting both sounds and sights of what was otherwise looking like a pleasant early summer morning. I tried to limit my prayers to just evening, or now, when on my pilgrimage to her, but the dream had prevented any further sleep and so I was tired, grouchy and more morose than usual. Had the sun just managed to pierce through the mist a little quicker, I would not have had to have troubled Him, as I am sure the undimmed beauty would have guided me alone to the answer, although this is of course also His work. It also occurred to me that I should not be so arrogant as to assume I know Him and His wants and that He did in fact want to be asked: perhaps this was why the mist lingered, enveloping me in a tired melancholy that drove me to direct conversation.

"What do I do Lord? How do I rid myself of this misery and her of her loneliness? Please, tell me what to do." I remember it as respectful, humble and of suitably hushed tone, but thinking back, was I not perhaps just a little louder, a little angrier and a little too helpless in my prayer? It mattered not because at that precise point, a raven landed close by and He spoke to me through this chosen vessel.

"You know what you must do. You have known since the day she died. It will be less painful for you this time. You know what to do. It's the perfect place for you."

The raven blinked, cawed and made to move off.

"But, won't...shouldn't...isn't this a sin...would it not be making it worse..."

The raven stabbed its beak into an unseen worm and swallowed. "Stop her being lonely. If you wish to be rid of this torment, then rid yourself of this torment."

It then flew off, soon lost to the slowly dissipating but still stubbornly lingering mist that clung to the surrounding ferns and treetops. But the mist was no longer of concern or source of misery for I could see regardless-clearer than had it been the height of August. He had given me the solution and I would start making my plans and preparations. As soon as I had been for my daily visit, of course.

By the time I reached her that morning, my mood was as elevated as the high,early-summer sun that, having fought off mist and cold, now ruled over all and shone as bright as it had yet managed this year. A few wispy clouds, aided by the slightest of breezes, were the only blots on an otherwise dazzlingly blue canvas and it was warm enough for me to remove both coat and jumper, even in the woods where the sunlight only managed to filter through in fits and bursts. Motes of dust in vertical beams scoured the woodland floor, awakening ants and other bugs. The birds' chorus was joined by a chattering of crickets and the occasional dozy buzz of a wakening bee. If I had needed confirmation that I was now on the path to solution, He had provided it, underlined and highlighted it for me: only a fool could not see that. I told her so, laughing at her whispered objections. Before I left, I knelt down closer upon the mounds of earth and crude rockery that I had chosen as markers. The earth was still beyond damp: a sludge that would require many a consecutive day like this to solidify. As I knelt, up rose a fetid smell, the only thing spoiling the otherwise perfect summer scene as even the flies and bluebottles seemed to only heighten not ruin this ambience.

"It's okay, my love. I have to go one more time, and then when I come back, I promise you will never be alone again."

It took me less than an hour to dig out a bed next to her and this time the task was more rewarding than onerous, though I took care to keep it as close as possible without disturbing hers. We sang together as I dug, this time more anthemic than funereal. After another shared prayer, I repeated my promise to her and briefly kissed the earth before leaving, knowing that I would only have to make this pilgrimage one last time, as soon as everything was ready- which I resolved would be no later than tomorrow, if not later that very evening. Now I knew what had to be done, there was little sense in any further delaying the inevitable and I just had to be brave. I plucked a dandelion and gently blew off its puffballs, hoping that as they danced through the woods and over the clifftop, they would take any of my remaining fears and doubts with them, so that they too could be lost to an otherwise indifferent universe.

I hated going into the village, let alone the nearby town that some grandiosely (and inaccurately) referred to as a city, though I was hardly one to judge them for this folly, often referring to my own dwelling as a hut. The swarms of people with their vile sounds and sickly smells always overwhelmed me to the point of a piercing migraine, yet today I noticed them less. Besides, I only ever ventured to such places when absolutely necessary and today was the most purpose I had been filled with since her passing. I tried to remember exactly where we had met that first time in this place, but the labyrinthine ways and constant traffic made it impossible to think, and it didn't matter anyway: there were plenty of other perfectly good spots to get what I wanted and desiring such symmetry as the exact same spot was pointlessly time consuming. I know you'll find this hard to believe, but when I was lost-when it looked like I'd never be able to finish my preparations- I swear this is when I heard, above the sounds of droning phone calls and angry vehicles, His raven calling me down a side street. Even if this was imagined, it led me to what I needed and I was soon back in the truck, ready to make things right. The late afternoon sun had given way to fat, black clouds that threatened to birth their contents sooner rather than later, so I hurried home as fast as the slow-moving traffic would allow. But once out of the city, the roads soon cleared. Few, if any, were heading in the same direction. I glanced at it through the rear-view-the last time I would see this place and I was so overwhelmed with relief at this fact that I actually cried, just as the first of the rain began to spill from the sky.

The rest was relatively easy as I had few possessions or arrangements to take care of: travel light and leave light had always been something of a motto. With my makeshift hut empty, I destroyed what remained, carefully put aside my few possessions in the truck and began my final journey to her. By then, it would have normally been more like the gloaming, but the furious rain continued to hammer down from skies as dark as midnight. The route up the cliff would be particularly treacherous, even without my heavy load, but it was at least not windy-and I could not fail: the possibility of taking a tumble this last time and ruining it all for her was the only fear I needed to spur me on, to heighten my senses, to make even steadier each step I took through the ever-sodden trail.

Marvelling at the contrast between the conditions now and that very morning, I had to stop several times, the rain lashing in my face so fiercely that vision was near impossible and my heavy flashlight twice slipped from my grip. Nearer the top, I had no choice but to drag my burden, before then realising that to continue to do so through the woods would damage it irreparably, so I slung it back over my shoulders and huffed on with gritted teeth and the steely determination and conviction of the insane, ignoring rainwater that somehow felt heavier under the patchy canvas of canopies and pushing to one side the screaming pain from both my shoulders and my left ankle that had twisted halfway up the cliff. I was close now-less than ten feet-but it was still almost impossible to discern any of my markings in that darkness, though at least less water showered down in this part of the wood. I shone my torch wildly, certain that I had somehow gone past it, and just as I was about to turn around in search of the cairn, my right knee connected with it.

What should have been agony was elation. The knee was either scraped, badly bruised or likely both-but who cared now? All concerns would soon be gone for she would no longer be lonely, now she had a friend. This one hadn't made anywhere near as much fuss, though the vecuronium would soon begin to wear off, so there was little time to waste. I groped for the hole I had dug earlier, threw in the burlap sack and ignoring what sounded like a raspy "Don't..." from within, unsheathed the knife before plunging it into the sack over and over, reddening the burlap with an eternal stain that reminded me of raspberry picking with Uncle Jack. From one side, out flopped a bloodied hand. Near the top, I felt like I could see the stains forming two perfect crimson eyes and underneath a cicatrice, like that of a jack-a-lantern. Uncle Jack had also taught me how to do that, amongst many other things that I should not have been made aware of at that age. A few withered and loose remnants of old tree roots flapped like tendrils on the side of the grave. I fancied that if I touched them, I might galvanise it back to life. That was the power this gave you. That He has given me.

"I told you I would not leave you alone, my darling. Now you are two, neither will ever be alone again. He loves you and led me to you to help end all suffering-in life, and now too in death. Sleep on my darlings and thank God he has chosen to lift you from the streets to His kingdom. Amen."

I properly filled in both holes as best I could, all the while watched by a lone raven who waited until I was finished before taking flight through the dark wood, this time heading away from the path that led back to the clifftop. With no other better idea, I soon followed after.

CHAPTER ELEVEN

OUT OF THE FIRE

By Denarii Peters

I don't suppose you know a good ritual for placating daemons, do you? I wouldn't ask... only, you see, I'm in a bit of a fix. You could say it's a matter of life and death and, even worse, I'm the one who might be about to die but believe me, I'm not looking for sympathy. I know it's all my own fault, given the fact I helped Lindy murder Jenny.

It all began last Halloween, a cold, dark night and a game in the woods behind the houses, a foolish, ill advised game inspired by an old book I found in my grandmother's attic. We began the rite by building a small fire, lit with matches stolen from the corner shop. All our families had central heating, no-one smoked, we didn't camp so why would we have matches in our homes? It was the first time any of us had shoplifted. Lindy and Jenny distracted the assistant while I picked up the small, yellow box from beside the display of "kiln seasoned logs". It was easy. No-one gave us a second glance. It was so easy I helped myself to a couple of chocolate bars on the way out as well.

We decided a ring of white stones pilfered from next door's rockery would have to stand in for the "knuckle bones from a recent corpse". Mr. Collins could always get some more stones from the garden centre. We weren't religious, didn't go to church, so there was no way to get either the holy water or the wafers. A bottle of mineral water and two Weetabix bars would have to be enough.

The ceremony required a sacrifice. It was convenient Mrs. Marshall's cat volunteered by getting itself run over the day before but when we got a close look at the mangled fur, we went off the idea of plunging a knife into it, left it where it was and I pinched my little sister's favourite Barbie doll to use instead.

By Halloween we were ready. I even had an old witch's costume from a previous year but when I tried it on it was too tight. I thought dark jumpers and our black school skirts would be gothic enough.

We couldn't meet until late because my family and Lindy's, like to go trick or treating and insisted we accompany our smaller siblings. Jenny didn't want to start things on her own, which was just as well since three was a much more auspicious number than one.

At last we had finished going round all the nearby streets. I was feeling a little sick from all the treats. There hadn't been any tricks so far that year.

It was almost ten o'clock by the time I was able to sneak out of the window. I suppose it's lucky we all live in bungalows around here. I had my bag with the matches, the doll and a fruit knife I'd borrowed from the kitchen. We had already built the ring of stones a couple of days earlier.

I hurried down the road and into the excuse for a wood at the end of it. There were no more than twenty trees in total but loads of undergrowth, long grass, nettles and the like. We'd cleared ourselves a little space right in the middle. You couldn't see it from the road.

The other two were waiting for me. They'd heaped sticks, dried leaves and some bits of an old newspaper Lindy had brought into the centre of the ring of stones.

We were ready.

"What do you reckon? Do we kill the doll first or get the fire going?"

Lindy frowned at me. "Fire first. That much is obvious." She looked in her bag and produced a bottle of tomato ketchup. "I've fetched some blood. I'm sure a sacrifice should bleed."

She was right. The illustrations in the book might have been in black and white but they did show what could only be blood and one thing was certain. My sister's Barbie was not going to bleed however many times we stabbed her.

It took all the matches to get the fire lit. It made a nice, warm blaze but we were soon scrabbling around trying to find more twigs. With it burning away at this rate we would not have enough time to perform our ceremony. Then Jenny explored a bit and found a dead bush. We dragged it over and the problem was solved.

Now it was my turn. I held up the doll and tried to stab it in the stomach but the blade bent and skittered over the plastic skin and straight into the palm of my hand. I cried out and dropped the doll into the flames, along with quite a bit of my blood. I would have clasped the wound to stop the bleeding but Lindy grabbed my arm to allow more to fall into the fire.

"Better than using ketchup!"

The doll gave off a terrible smell as it began to melt. Not quite the sacrifice as described but there was a body of sorts and there were more than a few drops of real blood.

Satisfied we had done as much as we could by way of preparation, we clustered round the book. It said we had to recite the Lord's prayer backwards. We were not certain of all the words but what we did remember from primary school would have to do. I'm not sure any of us got it all right.

We held hands, not a ring round the flames because they were now a little too fierce to get very close but we did our best.

As we approached the end of the summoning Lindy got the giggles. She let go of our hands and began to dance round the blaze. Her laughter was contagious and the final words, "And so, daemon, we summon thee!" were half drowned as she returned to us.

Our laughter died as the air turned hot. A sour smell, acrid with smoke, made us cough. I noticed the circle of white stones had been kicked apart as Lindy whirled around.

Inside the fire there was a twisting, a writhing. The smoke thickened and... a form emerged.

"Who summons me?" The voice was loud, the figure as red as the flames around it.

I could not speak. Looking at the other two I could see they were as scared as I was. We had not expected this. It had been nothing more than a game for a Halloween evening, like taking a step into a "haunted house", nothing intended beyond the delicious shiver given by the pretence of fear.

He stepped out of the fire. He stepped out of the broken ring. "This was meant to contain me, was it?"

"Go away, back to where thee came from, daemon!" Where had Jenny found so much courage? She waved her arms at the creature.

The visitor placed his hands on his hips and grew taller so he towered over us. "It helps if you get the words right, you know."

"We must have got most of them right or you wouldn't be here. We brought you and now..." Lindy stuck her chin in the air. "... now you have to do what we want."

He laughed, a deep rumble not quite thunder. "You didn't get anything right. You're lucky I don't burn you up. You have no control over me." He took another step towards us. "As summoning rituals go, this is the most pathetic and inept I've ever come across. What made you think an old Barbie doll would be suitable for a sacrifice?"

"We were going to use Mrs. Marshall's cat, only it was all messy and we didn't like the idea of picking it up."

"A dead cat?"

"It got run over."

"I see. Don't you know you're supposed to kill something? That's what sacrifice means after all."

I pulled a face. "We couldn't do that. Besides, we didn't..."

"Didn't what?"

"Well, Mr. Daemon, it was only a game. We didn't really intend to summon you."

"That's all right because you haven't. I've not been summoned. I just fancied a trip out. I often do, on Halloween."

There was something not right about all this. As I watched the daemon, a blob of red goo dripped from his forehead. "Is your face covered in red paint? Because it's melting."

The daemon's shoulders sagged. "Ah, it's the heat, you know. I'm not used to it."

"Not used to it? Isn't Hell hot?"

"I suppose it is. I wouldn't know." He raised his arms and long, white feathers curled up and around him. "I came to stop you doing something silly. You don't want to alter your ultimate destination, now do you?"

We stared at him, entranced, as the transformation from daemon to angel completed itself.

"Ultimate destination?" I frowned at him. "We've got lots of time to worry about that. This was just a bit of fun."

The angel closed his long lashed eyes. "True. At least two of you have the time."

I felt as if an electric shock travelled through me. "Are you saying one of us is going to die?"

"You are all going to die. Except for one of you, it will be sooner rather than later."

"Which one?" Jenny whispered the question before I had the chance.

"I can't tell you that. One of you will die for sure before she reaches fifteen. The other two could live a long life. You will know which of you it is when it happens. Survivors will be just that, survivors." He stretched out his wings. "I have to go now. Remember what I've said. Watch your backs."

He was gone. We were alone, watching as the flames from the fire continued to lick upwards and outwards, catching on branches and undergrowth, spreading, threatening to cut us off. We fled back towards the road.

As I ran I thought about his words. One of us must die. I have always been a logical person. If any of the words were true, they must all be true and I was sure an angel couldn't lie so if either Jenny or Lindy were to die now, tonight, I would be safe. I would have a long life to look forward to... but what if neither of them was the one? What if it was me? Could I avoid my fate by making sure the prophecy did refer to one of the other two?

We reached the edge of the woods but the flames still pursued us.

Lindy and I were a little ahead. She turned to me. "Wouldn't it be awful if Jen were to have an accident?"

"Yes, terrible. Such a shame if she didn't have a long life."

In this way our hurried pact was made and in the end it was so easy. Lindy put out her foot and I pushed.

Jenny staggered back into the encroaching fire, falling over a burning branch. She screamed but there was only us to hear her.

The funeral was a sad affair. We both cried. Afterwards we stood together in the rain.

"Perhaps, she did trip. It could have been her own fault. She never was good at keeping her balance."

I nodded. Lindy was right. Our friend could have met with an accident. We might have been mistaken when we thought we pushed her. It had all happened so fast. It was obvious now the angel had been right. One of us had died so Lindy and I were destined for long lives.

We drifted apart, saw little of each other during the cold months of winter and the heat wave of summer but as autumn and our fifteenth birthdays approached we found ourselves talking at break time, remembering the events of last Halloween. I suppose it was inevitable we couldn't leave it alone. Like the queen in Snow White, who has to check with the mirror she has succeeded in removing the threat to her, so we had to check with the angel.

There was little left of the stand of trees but we found a similar group about half a mile away. We wanted to get things as close to the way it had been that night as we could so I stole the matches, this time Lindy stole the doll and we brought a bigger knife. It took two journeys to fetch enough white stones. Mr. Collins would have to go to the garden centre again.

We were more careful with the fire this time. We made sure we cleared enough space for there to be no chance of the blaze spreading.

Lindy lit the kindling. It was odd. For a second I could have sworn I saw Jenny's face in the pale flames. I steeled myself but it still hurt as I pierced the skin of my palm. Six, seven drops or so was all I managed but I wasn't prepared to try again. It would have to be enough. The doll wouldn't melt all the way. Still whole from the waist up, it grinned at us, though its legs were gone. Once again it reminded me of Jenny, though she had not been grinning.

I took Lindy's hand and we began to recite the same ritual but only got as far as "Name be thy hallowed" when the angel appeared.

"I thought you'd be here." Just as last time he walked out of the fire, stepping over the white stones. "Only the two of you, I see."

"Jenny died."

He nodded. "So she did. Shame, that."

"We were so sad." Lindy scuffed at the ground with her toe.

"I don't know why. After all, you did kill her so there was no use crying, was there? Mind you, it would have helped if the right one had died."

I shivered. "What do you mean by that?"

"Jenny was never meant to be the one. You made a mistake." He leaned over us and his hot, sour breath caught in my lungs, making me cough. "Oh, yes. One of you is still destined to die before she is fifteen." He laughed. "I have no doubt I will see the other again in due course."

Behind him, the fire flared. Flames leapt upward and out from the stones. Above us a hanging branch, well out of reach until then, caught and more smoke billowed around us. The creature was gone and, despite all our precautions, just as last time, the small copse of trees was well alight. We fled, from each other as much as from the fire.

I keep thinking about how Lindy suggested we gang up on Jenny and kill her, how she tripped Jenny and pushed her into the fire. I am in mortal danger. I know I will be next...

...unless I find a way to kill her first. It won't be murder. It'll be self-defence. No one can call it anything else. Can they?

CHAPTER TWELVE

Treading on Eggshells

By Aneesha Shewani

Tapti got out of the cab and walked toward the apartment with a spring in her step. The October evening had embraced a slight nip in the air. The soon-approaching tranquil dusk uplifted her spirit. Autumn was the perfect season to spend time with a loved one, cuddling and watching a rerun of the web series - Friends. Tapti had finished her work earlier than usual and was looking forward to spending the evening with Ivaan.

She rang the bell, but Ivaan did not open the door. She gave him a missed call. No response. Her heart sank. "Not again." She whispered, knowing what it was. Ivaan was at it again and wouldn't open the door. Tapti rang the bell twice and then turned away, dejected. She walked down the stairs and sat down on the bench in the society garden.

Twilight gathered around her and brought a horde of mosquitoes, circling her head in a cloud, almost as dark as her mood. She sat there for quite some time, swatting away the insects and brooding over her relationship with Ivaan. Her thoughts were interrupted by the buzz of the phone in her hand.

"Hi, Taps. Sorry, but you can come home now." His voice was weak and apologetic. Tapti gave one final swat to the buzzing insects and her thoughts and gathered her purse and laptop bag. When Ivaan opened the door, she smelt strong bleach. She took his hands and saw all the cuts and bruises. His eyes were tired and glazed. Suddenly, she felt as weary as he looked.

Ivaan and Tapti had moved in together a few months back. They met each other at work, but Ivaan had taken a sabbatical to prepare for higher education. When Tapti started spending time with Ivaan in the evenings in his one-bedroom rented apartment, Ivaan suggested they live together. Date nights were becoming rare because Ivaan had lots of practice assignments after his morning coaching classes. Tapti liked his company, even if it was dedicated to a huge curriculum, and scribbled notebooks.

Theirs was a calm, domestic relationship - work, studies, web series, books, and weekends with friends or movies. It suited Tapti, an introvert, who appreciated the quiet life. Ivaan was a man of habit, preferring routine and discipline. In an ideal world, Tapti and Ivaan should have been married, but Ivaan was getting back to a student's schedule. They had to wait, and as it is with the young in love, even this seemed perfect against the backdrop of a clock ticking in the distance.

When Tapti brought her things into Ivaan's apartment, he was particular about assigning a space for her books, clothes, and other knick-knacks.

"The right side of the bed is mine. You can set your clothes in that chest of drawers over there. Come, I will help you." Ivaan was specific about the rules and expectations.

Tapti laughed when he told her, "In the morning, I will always be the first one to use the bathroom, and I will clean it up for you."

"That's ridiculous. What if I use it before you?" She teased.

"We will see about that." Ivaan had shrugged her question aside.

Surely, Ivaan lived by the clock and was up at 5:00 AM every morning; much before Tapti's eyes opened to a bright new day. Ivaan liked to keep things in a specific order and do things in a planned way. He was meticulous - from the way he handled his belongings, dusted the shelves, had meals at a precise time, or diligently followed his gym schedule. Tapti was definitely the messy one and sometimes Ivaan was exasperated by things lying around and not being at their designated spot.

"Please put the books back in the order you find them, Taps." Ivaan fiddled around on the bookshelf.

"Ok." Tapti said as she walked past him, balancing a bowl of popcorn.

"And please don't eat popcorn in bed."

Ivaan spent half an hour setting the books on the shelf.

"What's wrong? Is something missing?" She came out of the bedroom.

"The books are not in their right place," Ivaan said in a faraway voice.

"What's the big deal? Can I help?" Tapti felt she knew what was happening, but was unsure.

"Listen, Tapti, we need to talk. Okay?"

Tapti listened attentively and asked questions. He smiled. "No, it's not that kind of obsessive. I will not stalk you as a crazy boyfriend."

"Go on." She urged.

"It's just me. I have these repetitive thoughts about how things should be and the urge to fix and perform certain actions repeatedly. I cannot control these thoughts that make me do something. So, you see, I have arranged the books many times, but my mind tells me they are not lined up as they were before."

"Oh!" Tapti exclaimed.

"It is a condition - it is called obsessive-compulsive disorder (OCD)."

"Is there no cure?" She asked.

"There is some medication." Ivaan wanted to say more, but he let the sentence hang in mid-air.

"Let's go for a walk," Tapti said when she realized the conversation was over. She was now feeling guilty for not being careful with things around their apartment. She made a mental note to be more considerate, though it crossed her mind it wouldn't be easy.

Scratch, splash, scrub. Tapti lay in bed listening to the sounds from the bathroom. Ivaan had been inside for a long time. When he emerged, his face had multiple razor cuts, some still bleeding. Ivaan sat down on the bed, exasperated. He reached out to touch a fresh cut. Tapti cradled his hand. He looked at her with tears in his eyes. Today, Ivaan's well-laid out and timed grooming session had become a victim of his OCD. He had continued shaving because a voice in his mind told him to. Tapti knew he would now compulsively pick at the scabs that would form, and the healing process would be slow.

"I don't recall it was so intense before, but then I was not with him 24/7. Yesterday, he spent an hour arranging and rearranging the spoons and cups in the kitchenette." Tapti confided with her friend at work.

"I have heard about this condition." Shreya, her friend, responded.

"I feel helpless."

"Maybe it's the stress of the preparation for the competitive exams, or the schedule change, as he is now spending most of his time at home."

"Possibly." Tapti stirred her coffee, wondering what to do.

When a person's thoughts become triggers that control repetitive actions, and the person shuts off attempts to help, there is not much to be done. One can only painfully watch and wait for the phase to pass over; even when the wait is too much to bear and the obsessive actions are risky.

A scream escaped her lips when she opened the door. Ivaan was sitting on the window ledge in a precarious position, intensely scrubbing the outside of the air conditioner. They lived on the third floor, so this was a risky proposition. Tapti had gotten used to Ivaan's daily cleaning rituals and secretly she was glad for it because it kept their place spic and span. She did mutter under her breath about the weekend cleaning of ceiling fans and the top of the shelves, but she had learned that it was best to leave Ivaan to it. He did not need help. He just needed to do it. Interference only extended the process as the scrubbing and cleaning went on until he was fully satisfied with his endeavor.

During Ivaan's cleaning sprees, Tapti would get out of the way and go outside or just sit quietly in her corner of the bedroom. She sensed Ivaan's anxiety, and it rubbed off on her as well. Sometimes she would start impulsively settling her cupboard or peek into corners looking for cobwebs. His rituals were becoming a part of her life.

But that day, she was terrified.

"Go away. Go back inside the room." Ivaan told her when he heard her exclaim.

"Please step inside from the window ledge. This is so scary."

"Don't distract me. Go inside." Ivaan hissed.

She knew he was right, and she went inside praying for his safety. She nibbled at her fingernails in anxiety. Random thoughts crossed her mind. What if he fell? Would there be a police case? She started weeping and called one of their friends in desperation.

When they sat down together that evening, Manas spoke to Ivaan.

"Hey, listen, you have to do something about this."

"I know." Ivaan looked at his injured knuckles. All the harsh cleaning had caused nicks and abrasions. "I also know what needs to be done. I will go to my parent's place this weekend and start treatment with my doctor."

"That's great." Tapti was elated. Ivaan looked at her wistfully.

A quiet Saturday night, Tapti cuddled close to him, delicately tracing lines on his face. "Don't touch me, Tapti." Ivaan admonished. She was taken aback by his reaction.

They had always enjoyed their intimate moments in cozy evenings, even if they never flaunted their fondness for each other in public. As it is with the young, their days and nights were filled with acts of love and tenderness. Ivaan was a reticent yet vivacious boyfriend. He often gave her surprises and showered her with a lot of affection.

In all honesty, Ivaan was afraid to be alone. He craved company and liked to be surrounded by close friends. It was almost as if he was running away from his thoughts. When Tapti agreed to move in, he was relieved and happy.

It was reassuring for him to have her around. Her presence soothed him after he was exhausted and perturbed by his daily rituals.

Something changed in the past month. Ivaan was distant, especially in expressing physical affection. Tapti shrugged it off as the stress of his studies. Her intuition told her otherwise. She noticed he was calmer in his daily routine. His everyday rituals were still in place but contained within a time frame, less debilitating to his schedule and general well-being. "If he is stressed, then he would be more compulsive in his behavior." She pondered.

Out-of-the blue, it dawned on her. He had started the medication prescribed by his therapist, so it was curbing his anxiety and obsessive thoughts. "Was the medicine related to his repulsion to intimacy?" She wondered. Tapti started some research and even spoke with a doctor, asking for advice on the effect of the prescribed medicinal salts. The verdict was there - these medicines make a person frigid by reducing libido.

It was a revelation to Tapti. As a young woman, she daydreamed of a long life with Ivaan - of family and children. She started worrying about the limitations of Ivaan's condition and treatment. Without his medicines, he was hurting himself in more ways than one. On medication, their hurt was of another level.

"Is it the medicine?" She asked him as he sat there on the couch, waiting for her to go to sleep.

"What?"

"Are you not attracted to me physically because of the medicine you are taking?" She inquired without flinching.

"Yes, I guess so," Ivaan replied, looking straight into her eyes.

"Till when do you plan to take them, Ivaan?"

"This is not a course of antibiotics that I can stop in 7 days. You have done your research, it seems, so you should know."

"So, will we be like this forever?" Tapti's voice quivered.

"Who knows about forever, Taps! I stopped the medicines after I met you. I was a wounded soldier with disruptive thoughts that had taken over my life. Look at me now. I am more in control of my actions."

"But not in control of our love life. The distance between us is growing. Can't you feel it?" Tapti was choking on her tears.

Ivaan got up from the couch and sat next to her on the bed, caressing her hands. He cared for her, but it seemed an empty gesture.

Loneliness became Tapti's constant companion. She was fitting herself in the little spaces between Ivaan's compulsive rituals, study schedule, and evening regimen. They were only roommates now. Her life had become a ritual of just being there for Ivaan. Ivaan was a hard rock that she could not carve upon. All display of affection had fizzled out like an open can of soda - flat and insipid. They tiptoed around each other, walking on eggshells, each engulfed in their thoughts. They waltzed around in a strange symphony of denial and distance. Conversations were difficult; making love was impossible.

Tapti filled her days reading about OCD, attending a few counseling sessions for family members, trying to be compassionate and caring. She resented being on standby for a man with a rigid lifestyle and a stony heart. She lingered on, uncertain of her future. She wasn't sure this was how she wanted to spend her life. Then she marked the calendar.

It was 6:30 AM. The doorbell rang. Ivaan opened it to receive a bouquet of fresh lilies. He checked the card. It was a best-of-luck note from Tapti. Today, he was going to take the national-level competitive examination for which he had been preparing. He was hoping to get into a B-school for a management degree. He smiled at Tapti from the bedroom doorway. "Thanks, Taps. This is a sweet gesture."

"You will do well, dost." She pressed his shoulder and went to change for work, hiding the moistness in her eyes.

When Ivaan returned that evening, he sensed something had changed. The bookshelf had lesser books, the kitchen cabinet did not have Tapti's coffee mug and other utensils, and her designated clothes drawer was empty. He found a post-it note on the study table. It read, "Do well, be well. I have moved out today. You can call me." Ivaan held the note in his hand, but his attention was drawn to the faint glue marks from the post-it on the table. He winced and scratched at the mark with his fingernail. He went inside to get a cleaning cloth.

Tapti sat in Shreya's house, clutching her phone.

CHAPTER THIRTEEN

THE SELECTION OF A SACRED STRAWBERRY

By Bethany Taylor

There is something so sublime about selection, don't you think?

Having a box of chocolates set out before you, being told you can choose whichever one you fancy most in the pack. Maybe you prefer the hazelnut swirl, or the chocolate flavoured orange. Maybe you like the ones with nuts hidden inside, or a classic milk blend.

Me? I like strawberries.

Every time, without fail, I'll always pick the truffle first. I love undressing its rouge packaging, slipping the translucent plastic from its gorgeous figure. I worship its beautiful, hand-crafted form, carved lines sloping gently from the peaked top to its flat base. Before placing it in my mouth, I will utter a prayer, expressing my gratitude for the treat. This is my ritual.

And then I devour it.

I relish in how the fruity flavour explodes, melting onto my tongue. I can hardly suppress a groan of pleasure as the taste peaks, my entire mouth flooded by the sweet goodness. I have to close my eyes to fully immerse myself in all the sensations the experience has to offer.

But then, all too soon, it's gone. I swallow once, then twice, and by the third the strawberry has vanished entirely, leaving me with a dry mouth and a yearning for a second chance.

Never enough.

Opening my eyes, I stare down at the box, its colourful jewels luring me in. Deftly, I pick up another truffle, but a short cough snatches my attention away, back to reality.

"Excuse me," a voice interrupts my monologue, "Room for two, please."

Looking up, I find stood before me, a short man who can't be any younger than forty. He wears glasses with a tortoise-shell pattern and a coat I have no doubt cost a small fortune. Both of these, it seems, leads him to believe he has some kind of authority over me.

Beside him stands a woman. Unlike the man, who is painfully average looking, his partner is impossible to miss. A woman of around thirty-five, she is breathtakingly beautiful. From her shock auburn hair to the way she has elegantly painted her face, and the way she bats her siren eyelashes at me. Again unlike her counterpart, she is well-dressed, with a scarlet trench coat tied taut around her middle, putting the gentle slope of her waist on exhibition. Her coal-coloured eyes stand out brilliantly against her alabaster skin, which has been nipped red by the frosty air outside, and they are firmly fixed on me.

"Certainly, sir," I respond dutifully, and I begin to fumble with some nearby papers. Almost every single one of them has nothing to do with room bookings; I'm just trying to look busy.

Feigning concentration, then frustration and finally relief, I hand over the key to room 224. The keychain – a worn, miniature bowling pin, yellowing with antiquity – dangles alongside.

"Thanks – Alistair, is it?" The man looks at me questioningly, and for an instant I feel as though I'm being tested. I'm probably not, though; this is just another one of those wonderful human quirks which makes social interaction all the more draining.

"Pardon?"

"Alistair," he repeats loudly, then gestures vaguely behind him, towards the hotel's entrance. He elaborates, "the sign outside, it says 'Alistair's Abode'. I thought you might be Alistair, given that this seems to be your Abode."

He chuckles, but I fail to see the humour in his joke.

"I'm afraid not," I try to sound sympathetic to his mistake, but I've never been good at these sorts of things. "Alistair was my father; my name is Lucian."

For good measure, and only a little out of spite, I tap the nametag pinned to my uniform which reads HELLO my name is LUCIAN in big, bold letters. I take joy in the loud sound my nail makes on the plastic, though I try not to show it.

"I see. What an interesting name," he remarks, furrowing his brow pensively, adding, "Polish?"

"French," I correct.

"Fascinating, fascinating…" he says, and almost sounds like he means it. Without a prompt, he abruptly stretches out a skeletal hand and introduces himself as, "Bernard."

Unable to avoid it, I am forced into a handshake. The man's grip is so tight it feels as though my bones may shatter under the force; it's all I can do to grit my teeth through the pain. I'm liking the man less and less by the minute with his arrogant, forceful manner and how he keeps grinning like everything is wonderfully humorous to him. That is until he drops my hand to gesture towards his lovely partner, a segue which I am endlessly grateful for.

"This is Rosamund," he announces, and she nods sheepishly in agreement.

"Rose of the World," I translate. I offer her my hand, which she reluctantly takes and she allows me a brief, gentle shake. "A flower famed for its beauty – how appropriate."

The skin on her lithe appendance is supple beneath my fingers. Despite the outside cold, her palm radiates heat, and I can feel the fast beating of her heart mimicked by the pulse in her wrist. She appears so full of life, truly like a flower in bloom.

For the first time, I see the man's smile slip. For a brief instant, I think I can see the embers of an original personality beginning to glow behind his eyes, but this light fades as quickly as it arrived, and his rehearsed jovial expression returns once more.

"Thanks again for your help," he says, "We'd best get upstairs and make ourselves toasty."

"Right," I nod absently, stealing another glance back at Rosamund – partly to admire her, partly to see whether I can irk Bernard enough to reignite his spark. This fails.

"That means get warm, by the way," he elaborates needlessly, and offers a wink, "Just in case that means something different in France."

I can barely suppress the urge to roll my eyes. Somehow, this man is simultaneously such an overwhelming personality, yet with nothing real to show for it. I offer a tight grimace instead.

"Indeed, enjoy your stay!" I say in my best customer-service voice.

"Oh, I'm sure we will," Bernard reassures, then takes Rosamund's hand and leads her away to the hotel's iron-gated lift. The last thing I see is a glimpse of her copper hair as the doors close.

I continue my performance of a normal day after they leave. I file miscellaneous papers, take phone calls, deal with bookings, cancellations, queries, and outbursts. I finish the entire chocolate box single handedly.

For four whole hours I manage to stave off the need to think about that couple – that woman. But when the lobby falls into silence, save for the occasional bellboy rushing past with an empty trolley, it becomes unavoidable and totally, completely agonising.

My mind is polluted with images of her, standing in that red coat, belt tied tight around her slim middle. She looks at me with those eyes, dark pools urging me closer and closer. She beckons with a single finger, and my mouth waters uncontrollably. I want to undo her.

I haven't felt this way in a long time.

I want to know how she would taste. Would she share the same flavour as the truffles I consumed earlier? Would there be a similar explosion of sweetness? Would her fruity aftertaste linger longer than those chocolates?

I suppose there's only one way to find out.

I reach into a draw and retrieve my hidden switchblade. I observe how the silver glimmers momentarily under the warm lights of the hotel lobby before slipping it into my pocket. Abandoning my post behind the desk of my desolate hotel, I see the ghosts of the couple standing before me, and I follow their translucent footsteps to the lift.

Nobody is around, as usual, so I close the gates myself and press the floor number. A cold chill runs up my spine and my hairs stand on end as I see the button light up the colour of bone. The second the lift starts moving, I feel like I've begun ascending to heaven.

Hardly likely.

In my life, I've indulged in my fair share of treats: I've tried the easy caramel, dipped my fingers into her glimmering tresses. I've experienced the vanilla miracle, basked in the delicious, fresh flavour she leaves on my tongue. And the fiery dark cocoa who fights back, tooth and claw? I've had her, too. Once, and never again. Much too difficult to subdue.

The elevator dings, and I exit. Leisurely, I stroll past rooms 210 to 218, all of which I know for a fact are empty. This floor is always empty: I make absolutely certain of it.

This pilgrimage is not unfamiliar. Many times I have completed this walk, down towards the room which I now approach. It was last inhabited about three weeks ago by a young, naïve woman – all alone. That was the last time anybody visited this floor, except for myself, of course, and my most trusted housekeeper, Elijah. Since then, these halls have been quiet as a confessional.

Turning abruptly on my heel, I stop directly in front of room 224.

Inside, I hear a shuffling, like the sound of somebody pacing back and forth. There is a muffled voice discussing an unintelligible matter. I know it must be our newest patrons – Bernard, and his delicious Rosamund.

Unable to contain the excitement which bubbles over the edge of my brain, I knock three times, loud and in quick succession. The pacing stops, and so does the talking.

For the longest time, there is nothing. A terrible, boring state, the most torturous to live through, completely void of vibrant activity. Then I hear clear footsteps which ring out, the heels of dress shoes clicking on the laminated floor. Three strides, and the person is on the other side of the door. I can hear them breathing.

A beat. A brief standstill. I watch the doorknob jiggle as they fumble with the lock. Eventually, the door swings open, revealing Bernard. He is no longer wearing his coat, and the top buttons of his shirt have been undone, revealing the pale pillar of his neck.

"Hey – Lucian, right?" He says in an exceptionally casual tone, "Listen, it's not really a good time right now, Rosamund's sleeping. Is there something you need?"

"Nothing I needed," I confess and flip the knife in my hand, still concealed within my pocket, "I just realised – I didn't offer you a proper Alistair's Abode welcome."

Slipping the weapon from my pocket, I leave no room for hesitation.

There isn't even enough time for his idiotic smile to fall before I'm forcing myself through the doorway and stabbing him straight in the gut. I slit him open, left to right, gutting him like a pig. He doesn't even try to fight back, probably already in shock. Wide eyes gaping with surprise, he falls to his knees at my feet. He is still beaming up at me brightly.

Vile.

I pause only to watch him sway, observing how his eyes cross and uncross as his vision begins to blur. He keeps his eyes locked onto me for as long as he can, clutching at his open wound, gushing blood and staining his pristine shirt crimson. Finally, he collapses, head smacking against the hotel room's waxed floor.

One down, I think as I step over the man's small corpse.

Scanning the room, I see the usual décor: an oak coffee table, and mauve curtains which have already been drawn shut despite it only being six o'clock in the evening. The bed is undisturbed, crisp white sheets still tucked beneath the mattress, exactly as Elijah is instructed to do.

There are only two pieces of evidence that anybody has been in this room at all: one, a coat – Bernard's I recognise – laid out neatly on the end of the bed, and two, the mugs on the dresser. One has been drained of its contents entirely; the other has been left out to go cold.

I creep over to the bathroom, which is the only place Rosamund could be hiding. I ready myself, gripping the knife tighter in my hands, just in case she has some cocoa fight inside her after all.

But when I kick the door to nudge it open, the scene I find is not what I expect.

The floor tiles – which I know for a fact have been scrubbed clean recently – are covered with a layer of blood. The shower curtain has been torn down, like a great struggle has taken place. And lying there in the centre of it all is Rosamund with her throat slit, gaping open, already dead. Her coat is still wrapped tightly around her body.

Still beautiful, but quickly losing her flavour. Like barbecued meat served in summer.

I briefly consider trying to save her life, but something else catches my eye, and I am quickly pulled away from the woman before me. There, on the wall to my right, is a message. Smeared across the wall in blood are two words, left just for me.

BIG FAN

That's all it says, but it's enough to get my heart racing even faster. Instinctually, after checking I'd read it right, I tear out of the bathroom.

Bernard's corpse on the bedroom floor has disappeared. My victim, a witness, Rosamund's murderer. I am flooded with dread, naturally, but the strangest feeling overcomes me. I am delighted, too.

For the longest time, I had imagined I was totally alone. Nobody else understood what it was like; nobody else had their own ritual. I believed myself to be the last true artist left in a life full of pacifists and crazies. But, as it turns out, the world might be full of people like me – the people you would never suspect capable of doing such beautiful things.

And now, I've finally met a fellow artist – that bewildering Bernard.

CHAPTER FOURTEEN

THE RED FISHING BOAT

By Michael Noonan

Honor the spirits, but keep your distance from them.
An Eastern proverb

I parked the car by the verge of a road. I walked by an old gothic church on the outskirts of the town. I couldn't help noticing that in its graveyard, before a pristine headstone, a large floral wreath had been carefully laid.

Though describing itself as a town, Fairhaven was little more than an overgrown village that wound down a hillside to a small harbour. I made my way down the narrow winding road that led to the town, past the gaggles of tourists that mingled about the shops, pubs, cafes and guest houses, and at length arrived at the harbour front, which faced the North Sea. I was glad to know that the same seafront cafe was there, that Julia and I had entered, all those years ago. I made my way inside, went to the counter and ordered a cup of tea and a buttered scone.

THE SELECTION OF A SACRED STRAWBERRY

Twenty minutes later I left the cafe and noticed that the air was colder and that a darker and more menacing sky lowered over the town, as if to presage a storm. I fastened my anorak and walked along the quay. On the harbour waters I saw a bright red fishing boat, which looked as if it had only recently been given a fresh coat of paint. On its side was a sign, in contrasting white, which claimed it as the 'Aureole'. It coasted to the quay. One of the crewmen got ashore and firmly tied up the boat to a bollard. The three remaining crewmen emerged from the vessel onto the quay.

'Let's have a drink,' I heard one of them breezily suggest to the others. There were general murmurs of agreement and nodded heads. Then the four nonchalantly strolled towards me.

'Well you came back in the nick of time,' I said, in an amicable manner, to the first of the quartet; a blonde-haired man. 'That sky up there doesn't look too promising to me.'

To my astonishment the remark was totally ignored and the man, together with his three colleagues, breezed past me, as if I wasn't there at all. Not even eye contact was made. I turned and looked on at the departing group. 'Pardon me for being here,' I said, loud enough for them to hear the remark. But there was no response. Not even a backward glance.

I walked to the end of the quay, then back to the harbour front. I made my way along the promenade, then down some steps and onto the beach. I slowly and aimlessly sauntered along the stretch of sand where Julia and I had walked together those many years ago. Now there were only ghostly, fleeting memories and recollections to accompany me, instead of an actual, living person.

Gulls wheeled and glided in the dull sky. Far out to sea I could discern a bulky cargo vessel sat impassively on the waves. I kicked away stones, stooped and examined some shells, and, as in my youth, sent smooth and narrow pebbles skimming over the sea waves.

The air felt damp and the sky was overcast, and it was no surprise that a storm broke and rain poured down from the heavens. I pulled up the hood of my anorak and sheltered beneath the protective ledge of a cliff above which a cacophony of gull's cries could be heard.

After half an hour or so the storm slowly abated. Though it seemed more of a temporary respite than a full cessation of hostilities. The sky was still dark and heavy and the sea seemed as troubled and mutinous as ever.

There wasn't any point in staying there much longer. When we had visited the town, all those years ago, we had only stayed for a few hours. We had a snack in the cafe on the seafront, we strolled along the beach and back again, dropped into a pub for a drink, then set off elsewhere. It was and still is an attractive little town, in its way - sustained only by the tourist season and a declining fishing industry - but it had little to detain the passing wayfarer.

'It's not the kind of place where you can imagine anything happening,' Julia had said to me at the time.

'I suppose it has its moments,' I replied, before we trudged back up the steep cobbled road to where the car was parked.

Perhaps it was a bizarre, quixotic venture, on my part, in retracing the route of a holiday trip we had both made together, a decade ago. As if I could somehow relive the past, that was now dead and gone. The trip had entirely failed to live up to my unrealistic and fanciful expectations, and had been a dismal disappointment. I had conjured up no spirits from the vaults of time, and had felt no presence, or even intimation of my former wife. There were just vague, phantom memories that dimmed within the mind the more I sought to grasp them. All that was real was the grey sky, the strip of beach, and the endless, solitary sea beyond. Already I could sense the futility and pointlessness of the remainder of this trip. Though I was still determined to see it through. For old times' sake.

I would go to the same resorts we had visited, I would stay at the same hotels, walk along the same promenades, eat at the same restaurants, visit the same pubs, and go to the same amusement arcades; as if in the performance of some strange and elaborate ritual. As if I could, by some weird magic or sorcery, recreate some vestige or semblance of what we had both shared and experienced together.

Though I couldn't help reflecting that Julia herself, who was a practical and down to earth person – little given to emotionalism and sentimentality – wouldn't have approved of this singular journey of mine. She would have told me not to live in the past, and to get on with my life; and even, if I had the opportunity, to establish another relationship with someone.

Perhaps the past was an elusive, if not irretrievable entity; like a homeland from which one was in permanent exile, and with which no tangible contact could be made?

I walked back along the beach with the intention of going to the same pub that we had entered on that previous visit. I would have a drink, and then I would leave Fairhaven for good. And without even a backward glance.

The red fishing boat, moored by the quay, gently bobbed on the undulating waters. The door of the public house opened and the very four men appeared who I'd earlier seen disembarking from the boat. They walked past me again, while utterly ignoring my presence, as before. 'They certainly believe in making you feel at home around here,' I murmured to myself. The four walked towards their boat.

I entered the pub they had left. It was an old style public house, mercifully free of modern frills and trappings. Parties of holidaymakers were standing at the bar. Others were sitting at tables. I felt isolated and ill at ease, amidst that convivial gathering. Around one table a party of five local men sat, playing cards. They were dressed in the rough, no-nonsense attire of fishermen. One of the five was a tall, blonde haired man. He was curiously similar in appearance and build to one of the fishermen who had just left the pub.

I ordered a pint of bitter, and took a swig of the drink. 'Well you certainly wouldn't catch me going out to sea on a day like this,' I said, in a rather general manner, as if addressing no one and everyone.

'You wouldn't catch me going out either,' said the blonde-haired man.

I looked at the man, but he didn't return my glance.

Someone shuffled a deck of well-thumbed cards, preparatory to dealing them. There was a small pile of silver and copper coinage in the centre of the table.

'Well those four fishermen who left here just now seemed to have different ideas.'

The card dealer put down his deck of cards. All five turned to look at me. The bartender put down a glass he had been cleaning and learned across the counter.

'What four fishermen?' demanded the blonde-haired man. Though he didn't wait for an answer. 'We're the only fishermen in this pub.'

'But I saw them, with my own eyes. They left this pub, just as I was coming in.' I pointed towards a window. 'Then they walked down the front to where that red fishing boat is moored.'

'You must be seeing things, mate,' said the card dealer. 'There is no red fishing boat here. We should know that.'

'I'm not in the habit of having hallucinations.'

'What was its name?' asked the bartender. 'If you happened to notice?'

'Actually I did. It's called the Aureole.'

A strange, intense silence fell over the bar-room. Even the holidaymakers desisted from their talk and banter, and stared, with avid curiosity, at me, and the local fishermen.

The blonde-haired man pulled back his chair, stood up and faced me.

'That's not possible. The Aureole sank a year ago.'

'But it was there. As plain as day. Tied up to a bollard, by the side of the quay.'

'Let's see about this, then,' said the blonde-haired man.

I walked down to the quay, accompanied by the five fishermen, and we were followed at a discreet distance by most of the visitors who had overheard that strange conversation in the pub. I stopped at that part of the quay where I had seen the boat. But there was no sign of the Aureole, or the four fishermen, either at the quay, or on the waters beyond. The local men, and a good number of the visitors, eyed me with considerable suspicion.

I felt confused and bewildered; indeed, almost nauseous. 'It was right there. Bright red, as if it'd just been given a lick of paint.' I pointed at the swirling waters below the quay. 'I wasn't seeing things. They must have taken it out to sea again.'

'It was red all right. But how did you know about that boat?' one of the card players demanded.

I looked at the grim, implacable faces before me and wished I'd never mentioned a word about the incident. 'I only know what I've seen here this afternoon. I've only been in this town once before. And that was ten years ago.'

'Let's get back to the pub,' said the card dealer, looking up at the turbulent heavens; 'that sky doesn't look too good.'

The bartender went behind the bar while the others crowded before the counter. Another storm had broken. Rain water deluged down the windowpanes and beat a tattoo on the tiles of the roof. I insisted on getting in a fresh round of drinks, for the fishermen, in an attempt to create a more congenial and friendly atmosphere.

'What exactly did you see?' the blonde-haired man insisted.

I felt harried and fatigued, and paused for a few seconds to collect my thoughts.

'When I came into the town this afternoon I saw the boat, the Aureole, come across the waters to the quay. It was tied up there, and four crewmen got ashore. They walked down the quay towards this pub. I tried to have a friendly word or two with them, but they just ignored me. As if I wasn't there. I walked along the beach, and then sheltered under a ledge till there was a brief respite from the storm. When I came back I saw the same four men come out of the pub and walk along the quay to the same boat.'

'What were they like?'

I paused to think again. 'Let me see. They were tall, well-built men. In their thirties I should say. One of them was blonde-haired. In fact he looked rather like you.' Indeed the resemblance was remarkable.

The blonde-haired man looked at me, keenly. When he spoke his voice was slow and sombre: 'He was my brother. The other three were friends of mine. They took the Aureole out for the last time, one year ago to this day. About thirty or forty miles from shore their nets were snagged by the conning tower of a submarine that was out on a naval exercise. The boat was dragged under the water. All four drowned. They didn't stand a chance. It was a freak accident. A one-off. Perhaps you'd heard about it? It figured in the news bulletins at the time.'

'I may have done. But I had other things on my mind at the time.'

'I left a wreath on my brother's grave, in the churchyard, on the hill.'

'So that's why they ignored me? I thought they were just being offhand, and ignorant. But there was obviously another reason.'

The blonde-haired man stared hard at me. 'Who are you?' he demanded.

'I'm a Londoner,' I stuttered. 'I came here because my wife, Julia and I visited Fairhaven, on a tour of this coastline ten years ago. Just after we were married. We always said we'd come back again. But she died last year. I just wanted to see if I could relive some old and rather precious memories.'

'Why did you see them, and not us?' asked one of the card players.

'God knows.' I shook my head, and stared at the harbour waters. 'Incredible, isn't it? I was looking for something else entirely.'

CHAPTER FIFTEEN

KAVYA

By Andrew K Edgars

'Going back for countless generations, our village would gather after the end of the harvest. As a child, it was a magical day of celebration. I ate sweet cakes and danced. The other children and I played games until long after the sun went down. I would sit in Poppa's lap and hold my mum's hand while we watched the paper lanterns rise into the darkness. "We're adding new stars to the sky!" I remember exclaiming in wonder to my poppa.

At the age of eight, my mum started teaching me the symbols of the celebration. The sweet cakes representing our thanks to the land for the sweetness and nourishment it provides. Our dances, thanks to the wind and clouds for the rains that water our crops. While the children play games, the adults sing candle-lit songs of gratitude to the sun. Songs of thanks for enriching our crops and lighting our way. The lanterns, illuminated by those same candles, are sent into the sky to thank the stars for watching over our fields at night.

By thirteen, I was an expert at all things about the end of harvest celebration. I could recite every story, and did, until my friends and family became tired of hearing them. I reminded everyone I saw from the first day of planting how many days it was till the end of harvest. I couldn't imagine a pinnacle higher than being one of the voices included in the songs of gratitude. I pestered my mother into teaching me the songs years before I needed to know them. They gave me comfort throughout the year as I sang them to myself while I was alone.

That first end of harvest that I was finally a full participant in the celebration, I had found religion. It all made sense. The sweet cakes sanctified my body, the dancing my mind. While I poured the darkness and pain of the last year into the flame of the candles, the songs cleansed my soul. At the end of the celebration, the lanterns would carry all that darkness and pain with them into the sky.

Year after year, the end of harvest celebration brought with it reliable safety and comfort. As I got older, the celebration lost its luster. The stories became fairy tales and the actions routine. My heart longed to see the world, to fall in love, to find my place. I left for university at eighteen, leaving all things of home, at home. My husband, Ravi, and I met and fell in love during my third year of uni. After graduation, we had our wedding in my village and moved into a modest home.

Our first end of harvest celebration as husband and wife, I taught Ravi the history and its elements. I told him the stories and we laughed when he couldn't do the dances. We lit our candles and he tried to sing the songs. I reclined in his lap while we watched the lanterns rise into the sky.

Nine months later we had a daughter, our beautiful Mina. Having her attached to my hip allowed me to view my world from a whole new perspective. Caring for our infant daughter became my sole responsibility. I was made an observer of the daily lives of my husband, parents, and cousins.

Nearing the end of the next harvest, I watched my mum make sweet cakes with my gran. This secret part of their relationship belonged to only them. The next day I took Mina for a walk and found my uncle in the village hall replacing broken and worn-out floor pieces of the dance floor with my older cousin. In another room, a group of aunties with their daughters, all older than me, inspecting and counting freshly made candles. Outside the hall, I happened across some uncles and their sons, again, all older than me, making lanterns.

How had I missed this part of the celebration? How had I not thought about the hands that prepared for the end of harvest and to whom those hands belonged? Obviously, sweet cakes had to be baked, the dance floor repaired, candles needed prepping, and lanterns made. Did I think all these things just existed and took care of themselves? All my life, the celebration was just the elements of the day. I never gave any thought to the deeper connections that existed around it. My view was shallow, my experience skin deep. I missed the real magic of the celebration.

That end of harvest, I sat with my mum and saw her joy as the children ate her sweet cakes. My uncle beamed with pride at the dances on his floor. I recognized a sense of value and connection in the eyes of aunties around the room while we sang the songs with our candles in hand. My husband and I sat with our daughter in the grass and watched the lanterns rise into the sky. No longer did I see those lanterns as adding stars to the sky like I did as a child, nor did I see them as carrying away our darkness and pain. For the first time, I understood the lanterns to be a message to the universe that we were here. The people of our village, united in life, speaking with one voice into the night.

When Mina turned eight, I started teaching her the elements of the celebration. She was there every year as my mum, gran, and I made the sweet cakes. Seeing her playing while we baked, I remembered seeing my mum with her mum and gran baking when I was that age. Would Mina remember this part of the celebration? I watched with a deeper appreciation as my daughter ate the sweet cakes. Feeling as if, with every bite, she validated the time spent with my mum and gran baking them. I laughed as she danced with her hands up looking into the air, as if she could see the clouds to which she was giving thanks. She went off to play with cousins while her father, myself, and everyone who played a hand in shaping her world, and raising her, gathered. With our candles lit, we sang the songs of gratitude to the sun. I held her hand while she sat in her poppa's lap and watched the lanterns rise.

Bringing our daughter on to the next step in her journey with the end of harvest celebration awakened something special in her father and me. Nine months later, we had a son. Ravi, after his father. I'd never seen him happier than the moment he first held his baby boy.

The day came when Mina would be a full participant in the end of harvest celebration. To me, it was a magical moment to light her first candle and sing the songs with her. Mina saw nothing more than a simple candle, and said the songs were old-fashioned. My husband and I watched the lanterns rise without Mina that year. She wanted to watch the lanterns with her friends.

As time passed, Mina and I grew further apart. Since my mum passed and my poppa a few years before that, each end of harvest celebration left me lonelier than the last. When Ravi turned eight, his father taught him about the symbols and the stories of the end of harvest celebration. My husband didn't grow up in our village, but he embraced this community with the same fervor as he did my heart. It made me very happy to see him pass on the culture he inherited to our son.

The celebration of Ravi's thirteenth year marked the fifth end of harvest without Mina. We received a few letters from her over the years. Her last letter said she was pregnant and had married an American named Raymond. I was proud that she had made a life for herself but missed her deeply. Young Ravi, though, by the lighting of his candle had found religion. I could see so much of myself in him and the way he handled life. He loved deeply and worshipped the ground his Poppa walked on until the day my husband died.

Mina came home for the funeral with her husband and their two sons, Robby and George. It was an awful reason to meet my grandchildren for the first time, but the joy they brought me was like nothing I'd ever felt before. There was a week to go till the end of harvest, but Mina and her family did not want to stay. They had busy lives to get back to. Ravi was angry at Mina for not staying, but young men are known for their easily ignited anger.

During the dancing at that end of harvest celebration, a young lady caught Ravi's eye, Udaya. They had known each other all their lives but he told me, "It was like I'd seen her for the first-time mum." He was in love. They married before the end of the year and announced she was pregnant with their first child a few months later. She gave birth the morning of the next end of harvest celebration. They missed out on the cakes, the dancing, and the candles. But watched the lanterns rise through the window, their baby in her arms and Udaya in Ravi's. He cried when he told me about the "most beautiful moment of my life."

Cherika, such a beautiful baby. A brow like Ravi's and the lips of her mother. The smell of her skin reminded me of Mina when she was a baby. Ravi and Udaya invited me to move in with them. My heart was once again filled with life and joy.

Udaya and I would spend hours telling stories about our families, and our lives. I'd never had a friend like this daughter of mine. She and Cherika were the best gifts my son ever gave me. A few years later Ravi and Udaya had a son, Aadavan. And they are. Those grandchildren of mine, my sun and moon.

I sang them the songs of the harvest and told them the stories often. Cherika, my year-round assistant in the kitchen. Aadavan, the artist who kept the fridge adorned in works of beauty. Udaya and Ravi would prepare for the end of harvest with Udaya's parents, while Cherika and I made sweet cakes.

In time Udaya joined Cherika and me in the kitchen after her parents passed. What I had longed for in Mina, Ravi had gifted me and more. What I saw between my mum and gran when Mina was a newborn I now had. What I originally missed in the end of harvest celebration I now looked forward to all year long.

My daughter and granddaughter made cakes with me that were enjoyed by everyone in the village. Giving thanks to the land for the sweetness and nourishment it provided never tasted this sweet before. I watched the dances where so many had danced, giving thanks to the wind and clouds for bringing the rains that watered our crops. The children played while we lit candles and sang the songs of gratitude to the sun for enriching our crops and lighting our way. We placed our candles in the lanterns and sent them into the sky to thank the stars for watching over our fields at night.

For the first time in my life, I felt fully connected to my village. The joy that my cakes brought, the countless hours of time and resources spent on that dance floor, the homemade candles, and hand-crafted paper lanterns; I finally understand the why of it all. The routine, the ritual, the deeper connections that bind us together give life meaning.'

"That was my gran's last entry. She died a few days later," Aadavan closed the diary, grabbed the microphone, and stepped out from behind the podium. "It's been ten harvests since she passed. In all my memories of her, the only thing she loved more than the end of harvest celebration was her family."

He motioned toward the crowd where his wife and three children sat with Cherika and her husband. Even Mina had come with her husband, their grown children, their wives, and children.

"It is my honor to cut the ribbon on this new village hall named after the great woman herself. Complete with transplanted dance floor from the old village hall, just as gran would have wanted..." He paused momentarily, wearing a big smile, as the crowd responded in laughter at how apt the statement was, "Kavya Hall." With that, Aadavan turned and cut the ribbon, officially opening the hall bearing his grandmother's name.

What few pictures there were of Kavya hung on the walls of the Kavya Hall lobby amidst framed reproductions of pages from Kavya's diary. A statue of Kavya holding a small plate of sweet cakes stood in the center of the lobby.

Eight-year-old Sarah, daughter of George, became captivated by the statue of her great-grandmother.

"Gran Mina?" She asked for her grandmother's attention, pulling on her hand, "Will you teach me the songs of the end of harvest?"

Mina laughed before crouching down to eye level with Sarah to deny her request. She stopped to look up into the face of her mother's statue, her brow furrowed by the sting of regret. Her gaze softened as she turned, looking into her granddaughter's eyes, "Nothing would make me happier, little one."

CHAPTER SIXTEEN

The Art of Tapping into Fame

By Jay McKenzie

Tap tap tap tap tap.

"I can't stand it anymore," says Zoe.

Amman taps and Zoe rocks and Lorca squeezes his hands over his ears. I watch with my paintbrush raised, waiting to capture the chaos in glorious purples and yellows and browns. I like the colours bruises go when they're trying to heal.

Tap tap tap tap tap.

Round the room he goes. Five taps everytime he comes to a new surface.

"What will happen if you don't tap, Amman," asked the group therapist woman who comes on Thursdays. Amman, eyes wide. "I couldn't possibly imagine," he whispered.

Tap tap tap tap tap.

THE SELECTION OF A SACRED STRAWBERRY

The tips of his long bony fingers strike the perspex box that houses the television.

"I swear, I'm going to go mad," yells Zoe.

Too late for that, sweetheart, I think. I daub a thick midnight blue splodge onto my page where her face should be then press the whorls of my thumbprint into it.

"Tits," shouts Lorca, and I snort-laugh.

\#

In the beginning, there was nothing and then there was me. It makes me feel dizzy to think on it. What was I before? How could I not have existed?

"I need to know I exist," I'd say to anyone who'd listen.

In my one-to-ones, I ask the therapist, but she gives me science, and it isn't enough. The non-denominational chaplain who comes to visit talks to me of Gods and Allahs and Jesus and Buddha, but that's too much and it's too confusing.

"You were just dirt," says Amman. "And you'll get to be dirt again."

\#

The painting is as old as time, and time is as old as me.

"You held a paintbrush before you could walk," my mother would say fondly in the days when she still tilted her head and smiled. Now when we talk, her forehead wrinkles and she twists a polystyrene cup around in circles watching the scorching tea turn tepid.

"Art therapy has many benefits," the centre director tells my father. "We're so pleased she has taken to it."

\#

When Amman has tapped everything in the room and he sinks into the blue armchair, he closes his eyes, smiles serenely.

I wonder if I should take up tapping things.

"You can take your hands away, Lorca," I tell him. I want to paint his ears, but I can't see the shelly twist where they wrap in on themselves when his hands are in the way.

There was a poet called Lorca who wrote beautiful words and haunted Spanish hearts. Our Lorca says only rude words at completely random and inappropriate times. Zoe says he's stupid, but I think he's just tired of the beauty and the haunting.

\#

Once, the moon was a sort of purple colour and I crept out of the house barefoot with my pencils and pad. I wouldn't have been more than seven years old. The woods were dark, but I kept my eyes on the lavender disk illuminating the sky and loved the way the spindly branches reached across its surface.

Just a little further, I kept thinking. Just until the tallows framed the ball perfectly. It looked like Madame Riel's crystal ball from the travelling fair that came through town once a year, all glowy and held up by her thin fingers.

The ground at the perfect spot was mossy and soft, and when I let the earth caress me, I realised how tired I was.

It was hot when I woke, hot and dry, and the moon was gone and there was only Sergeant Herbert standing over me. "You're not a beautiful crystal ball," I told him.

\#

We stand in an orderly line for our meds. Zoe is just ahead of me, and I arrange my face into neutral to wait for the inevitable outburst.

"She's a bomb," says Amman. "A bomb bomb bomb bomb bomb."

He makes it sound like a cheerful ditty from a 1950s musical.

"What's the purple one for?" yells Zoe. "I didn't have a purple one yesterday!"

She did.

"You're trying to poison me!" She kicks the wall in front of the metal hatch. "I won't be poisoned."

I think the purple ones are to stop her from yelling crazy shit like 'you're trying to poison me', which is kind of funny in a sad sort of way. She shouldn't fight the meds and definitely not the purple ones. Never fight the purple. I like them. They make the edges of the world all blurry and fuzzy.

One of the new nurses touches Zoe's arm. Bad move. She starts kicking like a donkey, and I have to fight the urge to bray or they'll think I'm a lunatic like Zoe is.

"Come on Zoe," says the woman and Zoe growls at her, a tiger, an angry puma. Some of the older ones come and whisper nice things to Zoe, and she follows Marlene off into the Yellow Room.

"Bomb," says Amman.

"Bum," says Lorca.

\#

I made twig dollies in the woods and gave them names. I dressed them in clothes made from leaves and scraps of urban litter discarded by people who didn't care about the forest.

"This is my friend, Luke," I told one of the girls at school. By lunchtime, I was alone but cloaked in the whispers of my peers.

Freak.

Weirdo.

Luke drowned in the creek. I showed my grief with mud and hard-pressed graphite on the thin public school drawing paper.

#

Zoe always folds her arms at group therapy. She feigns nonchalance, but I can see that what she really wants to do is fold herself into an origami crane and fly away. I will make an origami Zoe, I think. See if they'll let me fly it out the window. I can make her fly away.

"We're going to talk about letting go," says the group therapy woman.

Lorca says, "shit. Shit."

Therapy woman nods her head as if he's said something deeply profound. "Yes Lorca. This is a good time to let go of all you're holding inside."

"Fuck!" He shouts. "Shit fuck!"

"Thank you Lorca. Amman, what is it that you need to let go of to make space for better things in your life?"

I'd like to let go of Group Therapy, and Zoe and not being allowed to use a palette knife, but I remember not to say these things out loud.

Amman taps his leg five times then his chin. "Hmm," he says, like he's actually thinking. "Hmm."

"He needs to let go of tapping." Zoe's words, sharp, short. She stands. "I can't bear the tapping. It's going to drive me mad."

The therapy woman says, "you'll get your turn, Zoe. This is about Amman."

Zoe huffs back to the chair. When I finally catch her eye, I tap the side of my nose.

"What are you doing?" she yells.

#

They gave me pencils and paper and I gave them the dark recesses of my dreams.

"Maybe try sunshine or a park or candy floss," said the wide-hipped, thin-lipped teacher. My paper, a twisted labyrinth of horns and fangs and thin, beckoning fingers.

"It's good," I told her. "You might not like it, but it's good, right?"

I was sent to the school counsellor, who flapped her arms and tried to Rorschach me.

Beelzebub.

Nosferatu.

Dagger.

Murderers at a bus stop.

"You know this has all been disproven, right?" I told her. "Fun though! Give me another."

\#

Lorca let one of his demons out to play last night.

The alarms went off at 4:44. The witching hour, they call it. His demons, or witch told him there was an assassin in the pipe under his sink and he managed to tear the basin from the wall. At least that's what Amman says. But Amman also taps things and says things and is most definitely a little bit insane.

It's a bit like the dream I had where a thick wisp of smoke lived in my sink, coming out at night to creep up my nose and soak through my pores. I made a sketch of it the other day.

"Look, Lorca! A sink demon," I said.

"Semen," he said.

\#

At the Institute, I became known as the creepy one. I'm not sure how, since Diane was using her own menstrual blood to paint with and Furla was making actual fucking potions out of animal entrails, but apparently, I was the creepy one.

"Where do you get this stuff?" asked the ugly one with the hairy mole.

I shrugged. "That's just what it looks like in my head."

I painted my dreams and my nightmares and more. My yearnings. They didn't like that.

"It's edgy," I said.

"It's fucked," they muttered.

\#

I ask Amman if I can tap with him.

He frowns at first, like I've asked him to dance naked in the meds line, then nods gravely.

"Everytime you get to a new surface, you tap five times."

Tap tap tap tap tap.

We start with the lightswitch, then the wall, the back of the blue chair, the bookshelf, the box filled with non-contentious board games, and the picture of two people hugging in a tree.

Tap tap tap tap tap.

"I'll kill you both," says Zoe.

I tap her five times on the forehead.

\#

I was first to present my final project at the Institute.

A plain jute cloth uncovered five dolls, each no taller than a Barbie, each hand stitched, rustic, lumpy.

"I give you Skerningvale's Murderdolls."

There was silence first, then a ripple, murmurs, nudges. This is edgy, I thought. I dare them not to fawn over this.

Each doll was wearing a perfect recreation of the outfit he or she was murdered in, during the speight of seemingly random killings that took place in our small community a few years earlier.

"You'll see that I have even detailed their fatal wounds and other injuries."

I was particularly proud of the way I made Victim #2: Shenna Guilory, only have two thirds of her skull intact. It was a painstaking task, lining up the shards of skull with the forensic images I managed to get my hands on.

"This is sick," said someone.

"The boy was my cousin," said another.

Then the yelling started and the night got sort of hazy.

\#

Tonight, I'm tapping with Amman, but instead of using my finger, I've dabbed my paintbrush in a pillarbox scarlet and I'm jabbing the surfaces with the paint.

Living art, this is.

There's something deeply satisfying about the thick blood-like blobs feathering off into smeared stains.

"Vagina," says Lorca.

"You'll get sent to solitary," says Zoe.

\#

They withheld my diploma.

When the principal - a loud Irish woman with crusted tooth enamel - called me to her office, she pretended to look sad.

"The nature of your work is highly disturbing," she said.

"But art is supposed to disturb," I rejoindered.

"We can't pass you."

I took my time standing, making my way to the door, turning. "I'll show you," I said. "I'll show you with my fame. I'll be remembered long after you will."

It was arrogant, sure, but having said it, I decided that it had to happen.

\#

They made me clean the paint off. I tried, but stubborn little russet islands still cling to the coffee table and the wall, and the TV box is now forever blushing in the wake of my art. Personally, I think it looks better now, but Zoe spat that Stranger Things looks even stranger through the smeary box.

Amman says they're going to replace it, but also that tapping it now is like tapping something completely new, so I'm pleased I've given him that. I wonder what he'll think of what I've done to it now.

This time, I've used purple. A violent indigo coats the hairs on my brush, and the pot in my hand is still half full of thick and ripe and plummy paint.

At the Institute, they taught us about the psychology behind certain colours: what we could make people see when they looked at them. I was delighted when I discovered that, not only was purple a prominent bruise colour and therefore a personal favourite of mine, but was loaded with positive connotations.

Nobility.

Royalty.

Luxury.

And my favourite: ambition.

I wonder if they'll be clever enough to spot that when they assess my Final Project, the fact that I've chosen to use purple.

I move to the doorway to survey the piece. In my head, I'm calling it Tapping into Fame, but I don't suppose they'll ask me for a title. Across the walls, the carpet, the ceiling, the TV box, the coffee table, the blue armchair and the ugly rug that looks like roadkill, are the steady, solid purple marks of my tapping. There's something quite beautiful about the way I've marked my trail around the room and they'll be able to follow my route perfectly.

Only one section awaits completion. I smile.

In the centre of the room, I crouch. I dip the brush into the pot and watch the gelatinous gloop of amethyst drip back into the pot.

Tap tap tap tap tap.

Slowly, reverently, I dab paint onto the surface, taking care to mask the red that would otherwise sully my colour scheme.

Yes, I think. Perfect.

This is edgy. This will make my name.

Zoe looks beautiful in death.

Tap tap tap tap tap.

CHAPTER SEVENTEEN

Unearthed

By Ramya V.

"Aunty! If you say, Mummy will surely agree and talk to Dad about it," ten-year-old Kavya, sitting on Maya's lap, pleaded to her in the cutest way.

"Kavya! You need not drag my sister into this," Dhara replied in an assertive tone.

Cupping Kavya's face into her palm and gently kissing her forehead, Maya turned towards Dhara.

"Akka! What is all this about?"

"Leave it, Maya."

Kavya's face was drooping with sadness.

"Stop the suspense and tell me what it is, Akka."

"Kavya wants to learn horse riding. They have arranged during the summer vacation, at her school."

"Wow, my sweetheart. Akka, why don't you allow it? It is a good thing and I am sure it would be safe as her school is organizing it," Maya's eyes gleamed in surprise.

"Maya, are you talking with sense? Don't you know about her father? He doesn't allow a horse picture inside the house, and you are telling me to agree to horse riding?"

Dhara spoke with uncertainty.

"Kavya darling. Don't worry, my cutie pie. Go to your room and play. I shall talk to Mummy and Daddy."

Nodding in excitement Kavya went to her room.

"Akka. Tell me what is exactly Akash's problem? Please!"

Maya was not ready to leave the topic undiscussed.

Dhara sat on the couch. She is married to Akash, a successful businessman for more than twelve years. They do lead a happy and contented life. The only thing that angers Akash is the usage of the word, 'Horse'.

"Maya. Once when I and Akash were watching a movie, the hero was riding a horse in the fight scene. Suddenly Akash got angry, switched off the television, and walked away. He said that his family has some curse over horses and his grandfather Rajamanickam died because a horse stamped him to death in their native many years ago. Initially, I did not pay much attention to it. But over the years I realized he holds hatred towards horses. Once he even threw Kavya's storybook outside the house just because there was a horse picture in it."

Maya, a journalist working for the Times of the Nation newspaper keenly observed her sister's words. She then raised her suspicion.

"It sounds so naive, Akka. Anyway, how about your in-laws? Do you think it might be some astrological belief?"

"I don't think so. His parents do not even utter the word 'horse'. They have strongly fed their fear of horses to him from his childhood. So please don't ever say anything about it before Akash. And Maya, please convince Kavya and make her join some art classes. I can't manage her during vacation times."

Dhara stepped into the kitchen and Maya followed.

"What is the name of Akash's native?"

"Thiruvengaadu. His grandfather, Rajamanickam was the only child. Devastated by his sudden demise, his parents left the village along with his wife and son, Akash's father, and settled in Chennai. From then on, nobody from his family has ever visited the village again." Dhara spoke as she made hot coffee for both of them.

After some routine conversation, Maya left in the evening. That night Maya Googled about the village. There wasn't much information, but it predominantly stated that Thiruvengaadu was known for its fertile land and farming was their major occupation. Dhara's words reverberated in her mind, and she felt something mysterious. In this generation how can a person be afraid of a specific animal? It did seem strange and weird.

The following weekend Maya decided to visit the village. She informed her parents that she is on an assignment and left with her cameraman Vinod. Vinod was indeed her best buddy. Without even revealing the actual reason to Vinod they were set for the journey.

After a night's travel on the bus and in the morning, they reached the place. Plush greenery on either side of the pathway welcomed them. They stopped near the tea shop.

"Looks like you are new to this place?" the owner asked them while preparing tea.

"Ah, yes. We are coming from Times of the Nation magazine. We wanted to click some photos of your village for the upcoming Pongal festival.

"Oh, please click our pictures also," he smiled, serving them tea.

After the quick refreshment, Maya and Vinod continued walking. The cold breeze even in the morning times was soothing as they walked admiring the beautiful environment. Maya suddenly held Vinod's hand after she witnessed something huge. Together their eyes looked at the magnificent statues that were about 20 feet.

A man with a lofty moustache holding a machete was seen sitting on a white horse surrounded by several horses made of terracotta along with a few elephants.

Maya quickly recalled reading about it. Vinod was already familiar.

"Did you get scared Madam?" he said trying to control his laughter.

Maya stared at him.

"Okay, Maya. Haven't you heard of the village deity, Ayyanar God? Many villages in south Tamil Nādu worship him. It is believed that he protects his people by riding on a white horse and sometimes on an elephant. People also believe that he blesses their village with prosperity and ensures they get enough rainfall and harvest for the year."

"I remember reading it online, but this is the first time I am looking at the statues in reality. They are magnificent. Vinod, click a few pictures." Maya replied with her heart still racing.

On their way forward, Vinod clicked the lands that had fully grown crops, ready for harvest.

"Hello! I am Thilaga. Are you from the media?" A twenty-year-old girl with vibrant eyes and a cheerful smile spoke to them. Maya introduced themselves to her.

"Nice to meet you Thilaga. By the way, do you know anyone who can tell us about the history of this place? We want to write a few lines as well."

"Oh sure. Come with me please."

They walked with her for a while and Thilaga stopped before a small, bricked house.

"Ayya*?" hearing Thilaga's voice an old man in his eighties came out of the brick house.

"Ayya. They are from the city and wanted to write about our village. I thought you could help them please."

Vinod and Maya greeted him with folded palms. He gestured for them to sit.

"My name is Thambaiya. I am very happy to hear about your interest in writing about our village. Let me share whatever I know."

Maya started recording his video.

"Farming has always been our primary employment. Every year the rains have never failed us and we would always have more supply of the harvest. Even when there was a famine in the neighbouring villages, we have never faced drought so far. You may wonder how. It is all because of the blessings of our deity, Ayyanar God. You would have seen his temple while entering the village."

Vinod and Maya nodded in acceptance. He continued.

"Following the harvest, on the full moon day, we all would gather in his temple for the thanksgiving ceremony. It is a ritual we have been following for several decades. Our deity would be covered in sandalwood paste. It is called 'Santhanakaapu'. Since he rides in the white horse at night to safeguard us, as a token of gratitude the farmers would dedicate a horse made of terracotta and offer prayers. All the horses that were offered would be kept in his temple. The celebration would be more grandeur than any other festival. It was not only a time of worship but also connecting and talking with each other, sharing happiness. A grand feast would be arranged and every one of us would volunteer to help in the arrangements."

"When is the next ritual going to happen? Can we also come and watch?" Vinod interrupted.

Despite the wrinkles, there was some kind of misery in his eyes. Maya noticed his reaction changing. With a heavy sigh, he continued.

"I still clearly remember that day. I was a little boy then. Many years ago our village Chief's son insisted that the horses that were offered should be made of wood and not mud. There was a huge commotion between him and the others. The villagers did not agree to it. It is against our customs. During a full moon day when the thanksgiving ritual was happening in full swing, he suddenly barged in. It was evident that he was fully drunk which itself was a sin. He along with a few other men threw all the horses offered into the waters. He had brought wooden horses which he placed in the same place. All of them left the festival halfway. The next morning, he was found dead in his land. Next to his body, there were visible shoe prints of a horse seen on the pathway that finally led to the Ayyanar temple. All of us believed he was killed by the deity himself for his arrogance. From then on, nobody came forward to continue the celebration. Instead, some of them still offer terracotta horses to the temple and have their own worship time."

Vinod was reeling in shock.

"Ayya, do you remember his name?"

"Rajamanickam! His family left this village after the incident. In fact, some of their belongings are still in their house. Nobody dares to enter there. Few of them say it is haunted as his spirit is still guarding the house. But I am not aware of any such thing. Maybe I am too old for all that." Saying so he pointed to an old building that was a few meters from their location.

"Thank you very much for your time, Ayya. We shall take leave."

Thanking Thilaga, Maya and Vinod continued walking.

"Maya, do you think we should write about this?"

Maya did not utter a word. She was walking towards the house.

"Are you crazy? After hearing all the stories, why do you think you are doing this?"

"Vinod! Do you believe it if people call it haunted? Haven't we written cover stories about such places in our city? Who knows, there might be some treasure. Let's just have a look. If you are scared, you are most welcome to stay outside."

Vinod knew Maya's grit and rigid nature. He followed her like he usually does. The doors were left open and the duo entered without any hassle. Amidst the cobwebs and dust, they managed to walk in. With some old photographs and worn-out furniture, the place looked quite empty. Vinod was trying to capture the photographs when he heard a loud thud.

"Maya, are you okay?"

Maya had stumbled over something. Vinod neared her. Together they noticed a portion of the floor had creaked in. Vinod moved the wooden planks aside. They could see a staircase leading downwards. Gasping at each other, Maya began to keep her steps slowly. It was dark and they switched on the flashlights in their mobile. In the corner, they identified some huge horse statues. Maya tried to lift one, but it was very heavy and realized it was made of wood. Connecting the dots, they understood Rajamanickam wanted these horses to be kept in the temple. But why should they be hidden in a secret chamber?

"Maya just wood cannot be so heavy," saying so Vinod tried to tilt one of the horses. It suddenly fell and broke.

Inside it was something white but covered in dust. Vinod tried to clean it.

"Maybe a sword?"

"It is a tusk," Maya gasped in horror.

They panicked. It was an unusual sight to see a broken tusk sealed inside a wooden horse.

"Maybe Rajamanicakm wanted to smuggle elephant tusks inside these horses and hence could have insisted on placing some in the temple to avoid suspicion?" Maya tried giving a conclusion to the story they heard.

"Makes sense. What about his death then?"

"Do you think a real horse would have killed him? It should surely be someone from the village. In a rage against him, anyone could have strangled him."

"Just because Rajamanickam wanted to replace terracotta horses, would anyone go to the extent of killing him? I don't think so, Maya."

"Vinod! It is not just some kind of replacement. Rajamanickam tried to change their usual process. A ritual is not just practicing a set of rules or processes. For the villagers, deep in their hearts, they believe in their deity with utmost faith and give offerings. There is also a psychological factor in it. When such rituals are conducted, it gives them a calmful mind and also the energy to continue to work despite their hardships in life. To them, a ritual means a religion. They wouldn't accept any harm coming in their way."

"Maya, did we really come here to take pictures of the farms and crops?" Vinod expressed his inkling.

Maya smiled at him. "We are getting late, let's leave Vinod."

It was getting dark, and they luckily boarded the last bus of the day on time. Vinod felt tired and his eyes were droopy. Maya's mind wavered if she needed to inform Dhara of her findings or leave the topic as last discussed. For one last time, from the bus window, she turned to get a view of the village when something caught her eye. Faraway behind the thick bushes she noticed a pure white stallion galloping at high speed.

Glossary

- Thiruvengaadu – fictional name
- Ayya – term to address elderly men

CHAPTER EIGHTEEN

Nityasumangali

By Dr. Gayathri Sampath

Traditional wedding songs praising the Lord were sung in the *mahamandapam* of the Thanjavur Brihadeeshwarar temple, invoking his favor upon the newlyweds. The usual camphor and incense aromas of the temple mixed with the delicious aroma of the feast being prepared in the temple kitchen, enhancing the festive atmosphere. Beautifully woven fragrant jasmine and radiant marigold garlands decorated the mammoth columns of the cavernous hall. It was easy to overlook the tangy smell of sweat emanating from the hundreds of villagers crammed into the *mahamandapam* amidst such a cornucopia of fragrances.

In line with the traditions of the community, the prenuptial ceremonies had begun at dawn with an invocation to Lord Ganesha and then followed by the various rituals of the wedding. It was now time for the concluding rituals during the muhurtham, which was almost upon them. The grand feast would be served only after the head priest declared all rituals had been completed and the wedding ceremony was now over. Anticipation of the feast was running high. As the vivaha homam puffed out yellow smoke, the temple's high priest led his congregation in a sonorous chant of Vedic mantras. The groom sat off to the side, unperturbed by the commotion. His forehead was painted with streaks of white *vibhuti*, yellow *chandanam*, and vermillion red *kumkumam*, and he wore a pristine white silk veshti with a red and green border.

Rukmini, Madhavi's mother, escorted Madhavi to her seat near the groom. The groom looked straight ahead, as all conservative Tamilian bridegrooms are instructed to do, and did not notice Madhavi, draped in the traditional muhurtham sari of maroon and gold, gracefully making her way to sit by his side. He did not comment on how beautiful she looked with her long hair braided with strands of jasmine and gem-studded hair ornaments, flawless skin gleaming after the application of the turmeric and sandalwood paste during the morning bath. He was not distracted by the glitter of her jewels—a ruby choker on her swanlike neck, a long gold chain, a thick oddiyanam emphasizing her petite waist, arms stacked with red and gold glass bangles, silver *kanukkal* with bells that tinkled as she walked towards him and diamonds on her ears that gleamed brightly in the sun. The groom also failed to admire her narrow dancer's feet decorated with symmetric streaks of turmeric and *kumkumam* and the intricate *marutani* design on her palms and delicate, long fingers.

Madhavi sat down in front of the homam and adjusted her sari, keeping her kohl-rimmed eyes lowered coyly. Yashoda, her younger sister, who was sitting beside her, whispered urgently, "Akka, he is here." Madhavi had spotted him when she emerged from her dressing room, but a painful pinch from her mother had made her studiously avoid looking at him. She shook her head and continued to look at the fire. People would think she was tearing up because of the smoke. The priest launched into a long-winded sermon about the significance of marriage and the roles and responsibilities of the wife. As he droned on, Madhavi's mind wandered to the day six months ago, when her fate had been irrevocably decided.

Six months ago

Fourteen-year-old Madhavi, her four younger siblings, and Rukmini had lived a quiet uneventful life in a small house on the outskirts of the village. The girls spent their morning practicing dance and the afternoons carrying out household chores while their mother attended to temple duties. In the evening, Madhavi accompanied her sisters and brothers to the temple to watch her mother's performance. Rukmini was a legendary dancer and often zamindars and dignitaries from the nearby villages would come to the temple to watch her perform. They would shower her with fine silks and jewels and insist on her dining with them after the performance. Madhavi was proud of her mother and aspired to become a fine dancer like her.

The fateful day had started like any other day in Madhavi's life–dance practice from dawn to mid-morning under her mother's critical eyes. "Elbows up, shoulders back, eyes straight ahead. Madhavi, focus on the beat and, for heaven's sake, smile", Rukmini barked instructions at Madhavi and her sisters. Sweat poured down Madhavi's back and her thighs and soles were on fire as she sank into a low squat, hands extended, finger curled as though she was offering flowers in prayer. "Hold, hold it. Feet steady.

Madhavi no! Look at your toes, they have to be straight out. Start from this beginning and do this pose again. Mind that you don't make this mistake again." Rukmini was an otherwise loving mother, but with dance, she brooked nothing less than perfection in even the smallest of steps and minutest of expressions. Madhavi and her sisters had been dancing since they were old enough to walk and were accomplished dancers, but certainly nowhere close to their mother's levels of perfection.

That day, like all the other days before it, Madhavi started cleaning the house while Yashoda and Mani had gone to the Cauvery to fetch water. It was then she noticed that her brothers Raman and Murali had forgotten their lunchboxes at home. Madhavi took the lunch to the school, as she was done with the household chores. Rukmini would return from the temple with rice and vegetables and prepare lunch around mid-day. There was time to drop the lunchboxes and return.

The school had welcomed a new headmaster a week ago. Madhavi's brothers, Raman and Murali, were full of praise for his innovative teaching methods and patience in dealing with recalcitrant and mischievous students. Madhavi had listened to their stories with amusement, glad they were finally happy about going to school. Her fate had irrevocably changed when she had smilingly yielded to her brothers' pleas to meet their new teacher. Unlike his predecessor, the new headmaster was young and idealistic, full of energy and enthusiasm, brimming with ideas to change the world. Madhavi had been smitten by his passion, erudition, and his ability to look past her lack of education and her background. He spoke of freedom and a new world order, where all would be equal. His words gave Madhavi hope, and she fantasised about a life in the future drawn by the headmaster.

After weeks of exchanging longing glances and secret meetings, the headmaster came to the house to meet Rukmini bearing gifts of sweets, fruits, and flowers. Rukmini rushed to greet him. "Headmaster Sir, what an honour. Why did you take the trouble of coming all the way here? I would have come if you had summoned me. Please, please sit. Madhavi, quick bring water and coffee. Headmaster sir is here," she called out, surprise and confusion warring in her voice.

"Rukmini Amma, please don't be so formal. You are like my mother," the headmaster replied with folded hands.

Rukmini said effusively, "You are too kind. Please tell me what brings you to our humble house. I am sure those scamps have got up to some mischief. Don't worry, I will punish them enough that they will never trouble you again."

"Err.. Err.. It's about your daughter Madhavi. I am in love with her and I would like to marry her," he blurted nervously.

Madhavi, hiding behind the door, blushed when she heard him say it aloud.

Rukmini threw down the basket of fruits she was holding and stood up abruptly, holding her hand out. "Headmaster Sir, stop this instant. Please take your gifts and leave immediately. I am going to pretend that you have not spoken," she snapped.

"But Rukmini Amma, I am sincere and promise you I will keep Madhavi like a queen. Why can't we be married? Is it because of caste or community? I don't believe in such distinctions," he pleaded.

Rukmini sighed and looked toward the door, where Madhavi stood pale and shaking.

"Madhavi is betrothed and to be married in a month's time. It is best you forget all about her. If you genuinely have feelings for her, please do not contact her further or you will ruin her life. Please go now before any of the villagers see you." Rukmini went inside the house and shut the door behind her. The master waited for a long time for her to reappear, before turning back downcast and disheartened.

Madhavi slid down behind the door, weeping bitterly. Rukmini sat beside her, stroking her hair and weeping silent tears. "My darling daughter, don't you know better than to have dreams like this? Forget him if you want to have peace of mind. You know you can never marry him," she remonstrated. From that day, Madhavi was forbidden from leaving the house.

The headmaster had persevered, continuing to meet Rukmini, hoping to change her mind. Rukmini had been patient, listening to his impassioned declarations of love for Madhavi and heartfelt offers of marriage. However, he refused to understand the reasons and explanations she gave him for not accepting him as Madhavi's suitor. She implored him to stop visiting their house, but he was not deterred, promising discretion. However, his repeated visits to Rukmini's house had not gone unnoticed. He was summoned by the zamindar and fired from his position. The zamindar's thugs had escorted him out of the village with dire threats to life and limbs in case he were to return.

One night, the headmaster had somehow sent word to Madhavi that he would wait for her at the station for them to elope. He had booked tickets to Madras where they would be wed, away from the archaic customs and conventions of the village. Overjoyed and buoyed with hope again, Madhavi had packed her belongings and was waiting for nightfall. She had put her siblings to sleep and was waiting for her mother to return from the temple. Rukmini was unusually late, but Madhavi did not want to leave without a last glance of her mother.

She saw Rukmini entering the courtyard, limping and wincing in pain with every step. Madhavi rushed to support her mother as she staggered inside. Her mother's sari was stained with blood and she could barely stand. The red dot on her forehead was smudged and there were wicked scratches on her wrists left by broken glass bangles.

"Amma, what happened? Who did this to you?, whispered a scared Madhavi.

"My love, go to your headmaster. I know he is waiting for you at the station. Go far away from here and be happy," said Rukmini, her voice breaking, pushing Madhavi away.

"Amma, what is this about? What happened? I am not going anywhere until you tell me what happened.", said Madhavi firmly, helping her mother out of her clothes, noting the many bruises on her back, breasts, and thighs.

"The zamindar and priest want to conduct your marriage next week. I protested you were still young and asked for more time. This angered them and then....", Rukmini faltered and burst into tears.

Madhavi helped her mother bathe and dress, put a salve on her bruises and gave her a herbal draught for the pain. Her mother slept fitfully, moaning in pain occasionally. Madhavi sat vigil by her side, leaning against the wall of the room she shared with her mother and sisters. Yashoda sighed in her sleep while Mani gently snored.

Madhavi came back to the present with a start as the head priest stood up and announced, "It is time for mangalyadharanam and the groom will now tie the thali. Please bless their union." Yashoda whispered, "He has gone, Akka." Madhavi nodded. She had seen him leave when the tray bearing the thali–two gold pendants and symbols of fertility, tied on a thick turmeric stained thread - had been passed around for seeking blessings of all in attendance. Volunteers were going forward inviting the guest to pick flowers to shower on the couple during the mangalyadharanam. Rukmini placed her hands on Madhavi's tightly clasped hands, hidden in the folds of the voluminous sari. Madhavi unclenched her hands and patted her mother's hands, assuring her she was okay.

She had no regrets about the decision she had made. It was the only thing she could do for him and her family. The zamindar had promised her that Yashoda and Mani would attend school along with their brothers, as long as she agreed to the marriage and fulfilled her responsibilities faithfully.

The head priest held the thali aloft for the gathering to see before handing it over to Rukmini. Rukmini hesitated imperceptibly before taking it from him and bending to tie it around Madhavi's bowed neck. The Vedic mantras reached a crescendo as the groom, Lord Shiva, in his abstract aniconic representation as a huge lingam, gazed kindly at his new bride. The hall rang with songs praising her new husband's kindness. For the villagers, it was a wedding to remember for a very long time. Madhavi was numb and did not feel the hot tears from Rukmini's eyes on her bare shoulders as she hugged her after tying the thali. With the tying of the third knot of the holy thread, Madhavi had renounced her past identity and taken on her mother's mantle in the Devadasi tradition. She was now a consort of the gods or Nityasumangali, the eternal bride.

CHAPTER NINETEEN

TO SIMRAN

By Bhavna Jagnani

It is September 2nd today, the day all of my friends meet. On this very day three years ago, we had graduated from college. Since then, we had decided to meet at least on this day every year without fail. Even though we have all completed our post-graduation and are either doing a job or trying to build careers in creative fields, we made sure that we meet on this day –even when we were out-of-station, pursuing our post-graduation, we would take a flight back to our hometown just for this day. Yes! This day was that close to each one of us. Even today, Rohan came by the early morning flight, after wrapping up his show the other night.

I go to the dining hall to have my breakfast.

"At what time will you leave today?" asked Mom.

"At noon. Ashish will pick us up." I replied.

"And return? As usual?"

"Yes. By eight o'clock, latest."

She nodded.

Time passed. At thirty minutes past eleven, my phone rang.

"Hello."

"Hello. Varsha, get ready by noon. I am about to reach Rohan's house," said Ashish.

"Okay. You've picked Aisha up, right?"

"Yes. I'm there in the car," said Aisha from the other side.

I was about to ask whether the phone was on speaker when I realised it must be connected to the car via Bluetooth.

"Okay. See ya," I uttered, and hung up the call.

I got dressed in navy blue jeans and a mustard coloured sweatshirt, and hung a sling purse which had an attached pocket for my phone.

At five minutes to twelve, my phone rang. After two rings, the line disconnected –meaning that they're about to reach.

"Mom, they're about to come. I'm leaving," I shouted while heading towards the door.

"Have you taken everything? Go and return carefully."

The question always is a rhetorical one –never requires an answer.

As soon as I reached downstairs, the car came. Aisha was sitting in the front while Rohan was in the back seat. Everyone was wearing sweatshirts of the same shade. I hopped in, and off we drove to the Amusement Park which was an hour long drive from my house. It would have been time saving, especially for Ashish, to meet directly at the park but then, there was no fun in it; and moreover, the promise we had made three years ago to go to the park together would get broken that way.

"How was your flight?" I asked Rohan.

"Good."

Listening and vibing to songs and singing along made that one hour feel not even ten minutes. We reached the Amusement Park and bought our tickets.

"Which ride do we go on first?" asked Aisha, after we entered.

"Is anyone hungry already? If yes, we can have something first, then go on rides," suggested Rohan.

"No. We will buy balloons first..." I said.

"Yes. And then, we go on the roller coaster. Then, we can have something if anyone feels hungry," said Ashish.

"Okay. Let's do first things first then," said Rohan.

We bought two balloons, one blue and one white, each and went towards the roller coaster ride.

Before getting up on the ride, Aisha remarked sarcastically, "You guys remember what to do, I hope."

"Yes, ma'am. Sit in the first and second rows, and the second it is at the highest point, release the balloons," said Ashish.

"And?" I added.

"I know what to say while leaving the balloons in the sky. Now, let's go," said Ashish, now getting a little irritated. He got irritated quite easily, that's why it was more fun.

Everyone was sad from the inside but no one let it out. We just tried to irritate each other to make all of us feel a little better, just as we had promised.

We hopped into our seats, Ashish and I in the first, and Rohan and Aisha right behind.

"Okay. So, here we go," said Rohan, as the ride started.

Two minutes into the ride and we were about to reach the highest point. We were all ready to scream our lungs out during the fall, at the same time to let go of the balloons and...

"To Simran." We all said together and let go off the balloons which the wind took directly towards the sky.

"See. She was waiting for them...woahhhh...," said Aisha.

We were descending –the steeping tracks were right in front of us. Oh, the fear and excitement that you have when you can see the ground approaching you at such a speed. We did scream our lungs out while descending, just to be clear; we didn't forget that. After another minute, we descended down the steps and on the ground.

"That was fun!" exclaimed Aisha.

I looked up at the sky. "I missed you." A tear dropped.

"We all did," said Rohan, looking up.

We all hugged each other in a circle. Water filled everyone's eyes.

"Okay, now. Remember no crying," said Ashish.

While the other two wiped out their tears, I held his hand and looked at him and blinked. He blinked back and troubled a smile. I knew he was trying to pull us together –it was typical of him not to show his emotions.

"What now? Another ride? Or lunch first?" asked Rohan.

"Lunch?" said Aisha.

Ashish looked at me.

"Let's go grab food." We put our arms on each others' shoulders and walked towards the restaurant at the centre of the park.

We took a table.

"Order, please," said the waiter.

"Uhh...Two bowls of noodles and eight chocolate cupcakes with letters T-O-S-I-M-R-A-N written on the pieces," I said.

The waiter seemed to be taken with awe but took note anyways.

"Thank you. Your order will be served soon." He went away.

"How's life going?" asked Ashish.

"Monotonously," I said.

"Nine-to-five job?" asked Rohan.

"Yeah. I'm teaching at a university currently. What about you guys?"

"Moving forward, one step at a time," said Aisha.

"Same," said Ashish.

"Me too. Trying to establish our names in respective fields, I guess," said Rohan.

"That's great."

I was the only odd one out in this group from the beginning; others were in creative fields –Ashish is a dancer, Rohan a singer, Aisha a writer, and Simran was into the field of photography, and I am into academics.

We were gossiping and remembering the "good old days" when the waiter came and started placing the order on the table.

"Your order, ma'am and sir."

"Thank you," I said.

Ashish and I shared one bowl, and Rohan and Aisha the other. After that, we took two cupcakes each and after finishing the meal, the bill was split. We took different rides and shot videos and hung about and clicked pictures for a couple of hours. The sky took its place in most of the pictures.

Around six o' clock, we started to head back towards the car. We sat the way we came. Windows rolled down, breeze blowing at our faces and song playing in the car, supported by honking in between.

Staring into the darkening sky, I thought about the day three years ago. The day started like any other day. The graduation celebration was to start at four o' clock. Boys were supposed to wear suits and girls sarees. All five of us decided to leave our homes by quarter past three. Rohan and I reached the college by quarter past four, went inside, and waited outside the Main Hall.

"Sad?" asked Rohan.

"'Cause it's graduation? A little. But we are gonna meet, maybe not so regularly but we will. So, it's okay, I guess. You?"

"A little."

"What's up?" said Aisha, patting our backs.

"Hey…you look so pretty!" I exclaimed.

"Look at you!"

A minute later, Ashish arrived too.

We complimented each other for our attires.

"Where's Simran?" he asked.

"I dunno," said I.

"Me too," said Aisha.

"Maybe she took some time to get ready," suggested Rohan.

"Wait, I will give her a call," said Aisha.

"Hello…where are you…–left the home late –okay, come fast but safely…"

"She is coming in five minutes…she is about to reach the corner of the lane."

We were talking, standing there, waiting for Simran so that she would click some wonderful photographs, like she always did, when she came. One minute passed…then two…when one of our batch-mates came running towards us.

"Si…Simran…" he started, panting.

"Yeah…she's coming in five," said Rohan.

He shook his head. "No…sh…she met with an accident."

"What! What nonsense," said Ashish.

"That's not possible," said Aisha.

"Yes...that can't be true, we just had a talk with her," I said.

"I'm...sorry. It's true. The bike...just met with an accident at the corner of the lane," said he, still trying to catch his breath.

We pushed him aside, maybe a little hardly but never mind, and ran down the stairs and exited the college premises. There was chaos all around. Down the lane, we could see some people gathered around in a circle. We ran and pushed through them.

All four of us froze. A car had hit the bike and Simran had fallen quite at a distance.

"SIMRAN..."

We rushed towards her. She lay there with her eyes closed. Blood had created a pool around.

"Simran...Simran, open your eyes," said Rohan, tapping her cheeks.

I checked for her pulse.

"I will be with my car in a minute," said Ashish.

"Her pulse is very weak –Simran."

We didn't have no time to wait for the police. As soon as Ashish came with his car, we took her to the nearest hospital. She was at once taken to the Operation Theatre and the doors closed behind the nurses.

"She will be alright, right?" asked Aisha, with tears running down.

"She has to be! Or else I will kill her," said Rohan.

(That didn't make any sense but you feel the emotion.)

We all sat on the chairs, holding each others' hands as tightly as we could with our eyes shut and lips moving in prayer.

"Please, God, we don't want anything else. Let the five of us stay together like we do in the phone's wallpaper," said Aisha.

"Yes, please recover her," I cried.

After about fifteen minutes, the door opened. The four of us rushed to the doctor.

"Is she alright?"

"Has she gained consciousness?"

"Can we see her?"

The doctor took his stethoscope off his neck.

"I am afraid she doesn't have much time. She has faced a massive blood loss."

"We can donate blood," asked Ashish.

"Yes, we can donate," said Aisha.

"It's too late for that. The accident was a fatal one. But you can see her for one last time. She is conscious but will not be for long."

We stood beside the bed. The tears were now bursting out from our eyes. None of us knew what to say. We just stood there, staring at her face with wounds all over.

"I...know...I don't have much time," uttered Simran.

"No. The doctor doesn't know what he's saying. You..."

"I want a promise from all of you," said she, cutting me in between and trying to hold our hands. "You won't cry after..."

"Please, no..."

"Remember...the Amusement Park we...used to go to. Don't stop going there and...and don't forget to send me balloons...and if you cry, I am gonna...come down...and haunt...you...guys..."

Okay, that did make us giggle a little but it was choked with tears. Yeah, she had a thing with making people giggle when they're crying. (She liked balloons a lot, especially white and blue –those were her favourite colours.)

"Please, no...don't leave us like this."

Her breathing rate increased. The doctor came running in but it was late. She had...

We were left there, crying our hearts out. We were still holding her hand.

"You can't leave us like that..." cried Rohan.

"Please come back. We won't irritate you ever again, we promise," cried Aisha.

I wished that that was possible, or at least that we had a time turner (like the one in Harry Potter) –we could have gone back in time and did something to undo the present. Accepting the loss of someone whom you never expected to leave, at least not at such a young age, is so difficult. We just talked to her five minutes ago...everything was perfect...

"Varsha..." said Ashish.

"How could she just..." I started.

The three looked at each other.

"Are you okay?" asked Rohan, putting his hand on my shoulder.

I came back to my senses. We had reached my home.

"Uhh...yea...yeah...I am okay. Thanks."

Rohan hugged me.

"Take care."

"I will." I hugged him back.

"You too take care. Bye, guys."

CHAPTER TWENTY

THE TRIALS OF MARCUS

By Emecheta Christian

Marcus has been living in the same tightly-knit suburban community since he was born. But unlike most of his folks, he lived with a big, boisterous family. His mother, father, and six siblings were chronic pranksters. They played pranks and teased each other relentlessly for fun. But there was one thing that brought them all together: the "No-Marrying Ritual."

The ritual was simple: whenever one of the siblings (or their cousins, who were also considered family) announced their engagement, the rest of the family would come together to perform a series of silly and embarrassing acts in an attempt to dissuade the engaged party from going through with the marriage.

It had always been seen as a harmless tradition that was done to test the potency of the love professed by the affected parties. When Marcus announced his engagement to his childhood sweetheart, Lisa, the stakes suddenly felt much higher. Marcus was determined to marry Lisa regardless of the outcome of the family ritual. But his family was equally determined to go all the way without bending the rules.

The day of the ritual came and Marcus and Lisa were summoned to the family's living room. His family, dressed in ridiculous costumes, began to perform skits and sing ridiculous songs, all with the intent to make Lisa second guess her decision to marry Marcus. Lisa, who was not familiar with this tradition, was taken aback, but Marcus reassured her that it was all in good fun.

As the night progressed, the jokes and pranks started to take on a more sinister tone. Marcus's siblings began to bring up old grievances while pointing out all the ways Lisa wasn't a suitable match for Marcus. Lisa, who had always gotten along well with Marcus's family, started to feel unwelcome and unwanted.

Marcus could see the hurt in Lisa's eyes, and he knew he had to put a stop to the disrespect. He stood up and addressed his family, telling them that while he loved and appreciated their traditions, he couldn't let them come between him and the woman he loved. He grabbed Lisa's hands and walked out of the door.

The morning after the "No-Marrying Ritual," Marcus and Lisa were sitting at the kitchen table, sipping coffee and trying to make sense of what had happened the night before.

"I can't believe they did that," Lisa said, still visibly shaken. "I thought they loved me, but they seem not to want us to get married."

"I'm so sorry, Lisa," Marcus said, putting his arm around her. "I had no idea they were going to take it that far. I thought it was just going to be a few silly pranks like it always has been."

"I don't know if I can do this, Marcus," Lisa said, tears welling up in her eyes. "I deeply love you Marcus, but I can't get married to you if your family doesn't accept me."

"Don't say that, Lisa," Marcus said, holding her tightly. "My family can be a lot to handle, but you need to understand that they love you as much as I do. Believe me."

Despite Marcus's reassurances, Lisa was still unsure. She decided to take some time to think about their future. The two of them decided to take a break from each other after Marcus's reasons weren't yielding positive results.

Days became weeks, and weeks grew into months. Marcus was beside himself with worry, unsure if he would ever be able to win Lisa back. He knew he needed to make things right with his family to have any chance of a future with Lisa.

He decided to have a family meeting to talk about the ritual night's events, and how they had hurt Lisa. His family was flabbergasted by his words, and they realized that they had been so caught up in the tradition that they had lost sight of what was truly important, Marcus and Lisa's happiness.

The family apologized to Marcus and promised to do everything in their power to make it up to Lisa. They threw a big dinner party in her honor, inviting all their friends and family, and went out of their way to make her feel welcome and loved.

To everyone's surprise, Lisa decided to forgive them and give Marcus another chance. She could see the love and remorse in his family's eyes, and she knew that they truly wanted her to be a part of their family.

The two of them got back together and decided to set a wedding date. This time, there were no pranks or rituals, just love and support from both families as Marcus and Lisa became husband and wife.

The family's No-Marrying Ritual continued afterward, but Marcus's incident served as a reminder of how important it is to put love and happiness above family traditions.

Regardless of what played out that night, the couple went on to have a beautiful wedding. His family understood that true love is stronger than glue and would always stick to the right partner. Even though Marcus's family ritual wasn't abolished, the love and bond between him and Lisa didn't diminish.

The newlyweds settled into their new life together and things seemed to be going perfectly. Soon, Marcus began to notice that something was off. He couldn't quite put his finger on it, but he could sense that his family was keeping something from him.

One night, as he was sitting at the dinner table with his family, he decided to confront them. "Okay, what's going on? I can tell you're all hiding something from me," he said, looking around the table at his siblings.

"Nothing's going on, Marcus," his mother said, avoiding his gaze.

"Don't give me that, mom. I know something's up," he pressed.

"Fine," his father said, sighing. "We didn't want to tell you this, but the truth is, the No-Marrying Ritual wasn't just a family tradition. It was a curse."

Marcus was shocked. "A curse? What are you talking about?"

"We found out that your late great-grandmother cast a spell on our family before she died," his mother said. "She wanted no one in our family to ever get married again after she broke both of her legs from a vicious fight with her daughter-in-law."

"And so, every time one of us fell in love and was about to get married, we would perform the family ritual in order not to attract the adverse effects of the spell," his father added.

"With you and Lisa, the curse seems to have gotten stronger. We've been receiving strange phone calls and mysterious packages in the mail. "We believe someone, or something, is trying to break you two apart."

Marcus was stunned. He couldn't believe that his family had been living under a curse all this time and hadn't told him about it. He knew he couldn't let this curse come between him and his spouse.

So, he decided to seek help from a local spiritual leader, who agreed to help him and his family break the curse by performing a traditional voodoo ceremony. After the ceremony, they all felt a sense of peace and tranquility.

The strange phone calls and mysterious packages stopped coming for the time being. All the affected parties started to feel happy and at peace.

The curse had finally been broken, and the family's No-Marrying Ritual has become a memory. They were all eager to experience the good things that the future held for the entire family going forward.

However, Marcus and Lisa's happiness was short-lived. A few months after the spiritual ceremony, strange things started occurring again. Objects in their house would move on their own, and they would hear strange noises in the middle of the night. They seldom saw strange shadowy figures moving around the house.

Marcus knew that something was not right and decided to investigate. He started to research the curse and found out that the spiritual leader who helped them break the curse was an ex-convict and chronic fraudster. He had not performed any real ceremony, and the curse was still active.

Feeling betrayed and imprudent, Marcus confronted the spiritual leader. "You tricked us! You didn't break the curse, did you? You took our money and left us in the same situation," Marcus shouted in anger.

The spiritual leader, with a smirk on his face, replied, "Curses, my dear boy, are not that easy to break. They require blood sacrifices and powerful incantations. To be frank with you boy, I saw an opportunity to make you feel good and also make some money for myself. I'm sorry to disappoint you."

Feeling weak and despairing, Marcus went back home to Lisa, who was now immensely terrified by the strange occurrences in their home. He narrated to her the outcome of his visit to the con artist and they both knew they had to find a potent way to break the curse as fast as possible.

They decided to seek help from a trusted spiritual leader, who would perform a real ceremony to break the curse. They found a reputable spiritual leader who was well-versed in African American spiritual practices, and he was able to help them break the curse for good.

During the ceremony, the spiritual leader explained that the curse was not just put on Marcus's family alone but on the entire community, and that's why many families in that locality were also facing similar problems. He also explained that the curse wasn't put by Marcus's late grandmother but by a powerful entity that was wronged in the past by the community and wanted to seek revenge.

The ceremony was intense and required a lot of consecration and spiritual practices, but after it was done, the strange occurrences in the house stopped, and the family felt a sense of peace and tranquility once again.

The community also came together to break the curse that was affecting all of them, and it was only through coming together, facing the past, and seeking forgiveness that they were able to break the curse and move forward.

The experience made Marcus and Lisa more dedicated to each other. They realized that no matter what obstacles come their way, as long as they have each other, they can overcome anything. The curse may have been broken, but the memories and lessons learned would remain with them forever.

After the ceremony, Marcus and Lisa's life went back to normal. They were finally able to live in peace, without any strange occurrences or mysterious shadows. They were also able to move on from the disappointment of being tricked by the first spiritual leader and were grateful for the help of the authentic one.

Things were about to take a turn for the unanticipated, as they soon found out they were expecting a baby. They were overjoyed and couldn't wait to start their new chapter as parents.

As the due date approached, Marcus and Lisa were getting everything ready for the baby's arrival. But, as fate would have it, their baby decided to make an early appearance and was born during a family gathering.

It was one of those typical family gatherings where everyone was gathered in the living room, chatting, and laughing. Suddenly, Lisa's water broke and the whole room went silent.

"Oh my goodness, the baby's coming!" Lisa shouted.
"Right now?" Marcus asked, looking around frantically.
"Right now!" Lisa confirmed.

The family quickly sprang into action, turning the living room into a makeshift delivery room. And amidst the chaos and laughter, their baby was born.

From that day on, the family had a new tradition, the "No Cursing Ritual" where they would gather every year to remember the events that led to the breaking of the curse and the arrival of their newest family member.

The family couldn't be happier, and Marcus and Lisa knew that they were blessed to have such a loving and supportive family. They were grateful for the lessons they had learned and the strength they had gained throughout their journey.

Even though they had to go through some difficult times, they knew that it was all worth it in the end, because they had become wiser, tougher, and even earned a beautiful new addition to their family.

As they held their newborn baby in their arms, they couldn't help but laugh at the irony of it all. They had gone through a curse, a fake spiritual leader, and even a spontaneous delivery, but in the end, they were surrounded by love, and that's all that truly mattered.

CHAPTER TWENTY-ONE

PERFECT PLOT

By Lisa Cortez

The first time I did it was quite by accident. To tell you the truth, the whole thing surprised me. I didn't realise it would be that easy. No screams, no scratches or trying to escape, and hardly any blood. There was nothing to clean up because it happened in the bush. The crime, as the experts call it: the happening as I like to call it.

But afterwards I realised, best not to examine your handywork too closely. Do what you have to do, tidy up, and depart immediately. You can check quickly for mistake but don't linger. First impressions are the best. If you fiddle around for too long, you'll mess it up, believe me. I gave myself a headache with worry that first time—fussing around and tweaking things. I was trying to get the right angle or something. It never turns out any better. That's my advice for what it's worth.

I guess there was DNA all over my car but since there was nothing to link him to me, I drove straight home and the next day, I pulled up my sleeves and gave the interior a good scrub. I also went to local the car wash where the manager, introducing himself as Joe, told me about their services. I chose the advertised promotion: FULL CAR EXTERIOR AND INTERIOR DETAIL.

'You are welcome to have a complimentary coffee, Miss, while you wait for the guys to perform the work,' Joe said.

'That sounds good,' I said as Joe ticked some boxes on a form.

'Would you care for the BONUS HAND POLISH?' he asked, looking at me with a completely straight face.

I raised one eyebrow as I contemplated the thought. 'Why not? Might as well go the full hog.'

'You'll find our services are very thorough. Nothing will be overlooked.'

'Er....that's good. It needs to be spotless.'

'Aha, going to use it in a wedding or something?'

'Yes, something like that.'

The fact is, after the happening, I panicked. Why? I've no idea, I guess I hadn't really thought it through and was a novice at this sort of thing. Since we had been close to the edge of the gully, I was able to give a mighty shove and the body tumbled down the hillside. I watched as his bright green baseball cap bounce off into a nearby tree. I threw a hoard of dead branches down, hoping they would cover the body, along with the rock, which I had wiped clean with leaves. I shuffled around to obliterate (I thought) my footprints and even took some dry leaves and covered my tracks all the way back to the car. I then drove my car to the other side of the road and returned to rub the tyre tracks away. The dirt on the edge of the road was easy to move about, being so dry and dusty, even so all that bending down killed my back. I'm a petite girl with regular visits to the gym help to keep my abs in good shape. I pride myself on my ability to lift heavy objects, but that night I was too tense and must have strained some muscle in my back (note to self...'relax, even during a stressful happening').

And then came the thunderstorm. No weather channel had predicted that rain. Nope, they all said, clear skies, clear night, no rain. Wrong! It did rain. At midnight, the skies disappeared under a weighty black cloak and when the cloak split, water descended in torrents, like someone left the tap full on. But I was home by then and fast asleep. I slept well, the tenseness had left me and I remember thinking, 'Que sera, sera'. I was pretty chilled by then. No regrets, see?

Now you can understand why I say don't fuss with the details too much, it's not worth the stress, (Look at me, giving advice, like anyone is going to commit to this type of happening!) In the end, rain had washed everything away: blood, my DNA, fingerprints, tyre tracks, shoe tracks. Jeez even that big bastard was wiped clean—probably cleaner than he'd been in a long time. My car had benefitted though, perfectly detailed servicing with polished exterior.

The second happening wasn't quite as straightforward, but I have to say, I learnt my lesson the first time. It happened a few months later and, again, I wasn't expecting it. This guy was quite nice, unlike Green Baseball Cap who had as mean a mouth as they come. Yes, at the beginning, the second guy was polite and friendly, and I thought he might also be kind. I did my usual trick; standing at the end of a road where there are no lights or CCTV cameras. I play with my phone, pretending to be busy. In fact, I am busy posting keep fit tips on my Facebook page or leaving comments on a movie chat forum. Somehow, those cruising dudes always know that I'm available. They drive over slowly with the window already wound down and call out, 'You free?' or 'How much you charge?' Green Baseball

Cap had yelled, 'Hey girl! You with the face like a smacked arse. You wanna make some money tonight?' I admit that made my blood boil. I should have said, 'Piss off', but I meekly smiled back at him. I wanted to see how far I would go, that night.

The second guy was kind and hesitant. He said, 'Excuse me, Miss. Are you available to make an old man happy?' He wasn't really old, maybe around 50. I looked him over. From what I could see he was well-groomed and had a pleasant round face.

I said, 'Certainly sir. I can bring you ten minutes of delight for $40—but tonight for only sixty dollars, I am offering you a twenty-minute promotion, the PLEASURE PLUS PACK.' I know few can resist a bargain, especially when I mention a secret location.

Of course he asked for the special, so I had him walk over to my car which was hidden around the back of the building. I kept him relaxed with my banter about the perfect spot with a great view that will blow his mind, along with my special techniques. It is only a five minutes' drive out of town to the bushland location I usually frequent. At the front of the vacant block, stood a For Sale sign.

Land for sale. Scenic views, virgin bush. Mainly level block, several good building sites. Call Jenny at Perfect Real Estate.

Yep, perfect block, perfect spot.

I always reassure my clients that the 20 minutes doesn't start until I undo their belt. I lead them onto the block, past the sign and into the dense bush. Well Mr Old-but-not-so-old-handsome-and-well-groomed seemed pleased with the arrangement, and certainly enjoyed the services I provided. But then to my surprise, he wanted to renege on the deal. He got very nasty.

'You think just because you got some cum on your face, you did something special?' he snarled at me. I didn't reply. We were walking back to the car and I could sense he wanted to frighten me. It didn't work. I wasn't even mad at him, just disappointed.

'Calm down,' I said turning my back on him. 'You got exactly what you asked for.'

He opened his mouth and out came some very strong expletives. He grabbed me by the arm and jerked me around to face him. He was short and a little podgy; not tall and muscular like the first one. I knew what I had to do. I was prepared.

'You seem like a smart guy,' I said. 'I want to show you an interesting phenomenon'.

That got his attention. He followed me, still gripping my arm. I walked towards this large tree where I leaned up again the trunk and put my free hand down. The rough bark scraped my fingertips. I found the solid length of wood I'd left positioned there.

'Look at the sky, over beyond those trees, can you see it?' I whispered as if it was something extraordinary. Of course, he couldn't see it, though he peered into the distance where a sliver of moonlight was illuminating the tops of trees. He turned around to tell me what a "fucking bitch" I was, but before he could finish the words, I had whacked him squarely on the back of the head. Good shot too. His mouth formed into a perfect O as he let out several long banshee-type screeches. He staggered and fell, clutching the back of his head where blood was spurting. I moved to avoid it and waited until he was quite done. I just left him where he fell, blood and all. Didn't bother covering him up or tipping him over the edge of the gully. Back at the car, I placed the plank of wood in one of the orange bin bags I keep in the boot. If someone found him tomorrow, so be it, I thought. The police would be disappointed not to find the weapon.

But the body wasn't found for weeks. Foxes and vermin had got to it, so I'm not sure what forensics had to work with. Frankly, I was past caring and glad I hadn't fussed around but gone straight home to bed that night. Do you see what I mean?

Green Baseball Cap was found a few days after the happening, but he was squeaky clean as I've explained. I won't reveal what the bastard guy did to me that night. Not pretty. He definitely got what he deserved. He never saw it coming. He would only have felt the sharp blow of the rock to his head—very quick and painless. Unlike what he put me through. Still, I owe him. It was thanks to him, that first time, that I perfected my handiwork. The wood required a couple of whacks but was easier to manage than the rock which had cut my hand and given me cramps in my fingers.

Over the next couple of years, I had a few more happenings but later I became so chilled, I rarely needed to go the whole way. The guys must have sensed they were in danger and pulled their heads in real quick. Those that didn't, well, they are still missing. A few ended up down that gully and were never found—some poor wife is wondering to this day what happened to her hubby.

It might seem strange to you, but I never analyzed what that period in my life signified. Anyway, I have well and truly retired from that line of work now, so it's pointless even to speculate.

I had had my eye on Joe from the first time he offered me such good customer service. We got to chatting each time I brought my car in, and then we started dating. I wasn't looking to settle down, but he seemed a hardworking and decent sort. When he proposed we buy some land and build a house, get a dog and maybe some chickens, I thought, why the hell not? So we bought that vacant block in the bush. Funny thing: it was still for sale. Jenny, the Perfect Real Estate agent never disclosed any of its disturbing histories, though she must have known (it was all over the news at the time). She was dead right about the scenic views and virgin bush. Turned out to be twenty acres of undulating land, and as advertised there were several decent building sites to choose from. We created a long winding driveway away from the bushland and built our home on a hilltop.

Once a year, the dog and I walk down to that small corner by the main road, to visit my special tree and the happenings' location. It's like a yearly homecoming ritual and we both enjoy it. I inspect the area carefully, peering into the gully, touching the tree; paying homage to the secrets the land is hiding under its fecund mantel of earth, foliage, and dust. The dog shuffles around in the dirt and leaves his scent on every tree. But, as hard as I try, I never find any remnants of those happenings except in my memory, and that is fading year by year.

But it is a happy memory, don't you know it?

CHAPTER TWENTY-TWO

THE RITUAL OF THE RED MOON

By Prosper Ugbosu-Joe

It was a dark and stormy night, the kind that made you want to curl up with a good book and a warm cup of cocoa. But I was not so lucky. I had to work the night shift at the gas station, a job I hated with a passion.

As I sat behind the counter, trying to pass the time by reading an old magazine, I couldn't help but feel a sense of unease. The atmosphere outside was thick with tension, and the red moon that hung low in the sky seemed to be mocking me with its eerie glow.

Just as I was starting to doze off, the bell above the door jingled, signaling the arrival of a customer. I looked up, expecting to see a tired trucker or a local resident coming in for some snacks.

But what I saw instead was a figure shrouded in darkness, its face hidden by a hooded cloak. I froze, my heart pounding in my chest as the figure approached the counter.

"Can I help you?" I asked, my voice shaking slightly.

The figure didn't answer, but instead reached into its pocket and pulled out a small, intricately carved wooden box. It placed the box on the counter, then turned and walked out of the store without a word.

I was too stunned to move, and by the time I had gathered my wits, the figure was gone. I stood there for a moment, wondering what the hell had just happened.

Finally, I mustered up the courage to approach the box. As I lifted the lid, a bright light burst forth, blinding me. When my vision cleared, I saw that the box was empty.

I had no idea what the strange occurrence meant, but I knew one thing for sure: I would never forget the night of the red moon.

But the strangeness didn't end there. As the night wore on, more and more unusual events occurred. A group of teenagers came in, ranting about seeing a ghost in the park. An old man claimed he had been visited by extraterrestrial beings. And even the weather seemed to be against me, as the storm outside raged on with a ferocity I had never seen before.

I tried to brush it all off as coincidence, but deep down I couldn't shake the feeling that something sinister was at play. As I counted down the minutes until my shift was over, I couldn't help but wonder what other strange occurrences the night had in store.

As the first rays of dawn broke through the clouds, the storm finally dissipated and the red moon faded from the sky. The sense of unease that had weighed on me all night lifted, and I breathed a sigh of relief.

But even as I locked up the gas station and headed home, I couldn't shake the feeling that something was still off. The events of the night stayed with me, haunting me like a bad dream. And as I drifted off to sleep, I couldn't help but wonder if the strange occurrences were over, or if they were just the beginning.

As I sat in my living room, surrounded by candles, crystals, and various other ritual items, I couldn't help but feel a sense of nervous excitement. After the strange occurrences on the night of the red moon, I had done some research and discovered that there was a way to uncover the truth behind what had happened.

The process was risky, but I was determined to find out what was going on. And so, with the help of a small group of friends who were just as curious as I was, I had set out to perform a ritual that would allow us to communicate with the spirits and uncover the truth.

We had spent hours gathering the necessary items, making sure that everything was perfect. We had even consulted a local spiritualist to make sure we were doing everything correctly.

As the last of the candles was lit and the crystals were carefully placed around the circle, I couldn't help but feel a sense of nervous anticipation. This was it. We were about to embark on a journey that would reveal the truth behind the strange occurrences on the night of the red moon.

With a deep breath, I began the ritual, chanting the ancient words that would open the portal to the spirit world. As the energy in the room began to shift, I knew that we were about to uncover the truth, no matter what it might be.

As the ritual reached its climax, the energy in the room became almost palpable. I could feel the spirits gathering around us, their presence almost palpable. And then, as if in a trance, I began to speak.

The words that came out of my mouth were not my own, but rather the words of the spirits. They told us of a dark force that had been unleashed on the night of the red moon, a force that had been causing the strange occurrences around town.

My friends and I listened in horror as the spirits revealed the true nature of the dark force. It was a being of pure malevolence, one that fed on the fear and chaos it had caused.

But the spirits didn't stop there. They also gave us a way to defeat the dark force and banish it back to the spirit realm. It would require a great sacrifice, but we were willing to do whatever it took to stop the chaos.

And so, with the help of the spirits, we performed the final ritual, banishing the dark force back to where it belonged. As the portal closed, the strange occurrences ceased, and the town returned to normal.

I never forgot the night of the red moon, and the strange occurrences that had plagued our town. But I also knew that we had saved the day, thanks to the help of the spirits and the bravery of my friends. It was a night I would never forget, and one that had forever changed my life.

As the sun set on the small village, the air was thick with anticipation. For weeks, my ancestors and I had been preparing for this moment, gathering the necessary items and rehearsing the ancient rituals.

Tonight was the night of the full moon, and we were going to invoke the spirits of our ancestors. It was a sacred ceremony, one that had been passed down through the generations.

As the fire was lit and the drums began to beat, I could feel the energy in the air shifting. The spirits were gathering, drawn to the ceremony like moths to a flame.

I took my place at the head of the circle, surrounded by my ancestors and the other members of the village. As I began the incantation, the spirits began to manifest themselves, taking on physical form before our very eyes.

The ceremony lasted for hours, as we danced and sang and invoked the spirits of our ancestors. They shared their wisdom and stories with us, and we were filled with a sense of pride and connection to our past.

As the moon began to set and the ceremony came to a close, I felt a sense of peace wash over me. The spirits had been pleased, and we had successfully connected with our ancestors.

It was a night I would never forget, and one that had deepened my connection to my heritage and the spirits that surrounded us.

As we gathered up the ritual items and prepared to go our separate ways, I couldn't help but feel grateful for the experience. The ceremony had been truly transformative, and I knew that it would stay with me for the rest of my life.

But as we made our way back to our homes, a sense of unease began to creep over me. I couldn't shake the feeling that something was off, that there was an energy in the air that was not quite right.

As we entered the village, I saw that all of the lights were off and the streets were eerily quiet. It was as if the entire town had been abandoned.

My ancestors and I exchanged worried glances, and I knew that we had to do something. We couldn't just leave the town to whatever fate had befallen it.

And so, with the help of the spirits we had invoked earlier, we set out to uncover the truth behind the strange occurrences that had befallen our town. It was a long and dangerous journey, but in the end, we were able to vanquish the evil that had threatened our home and restore balance to the land.

As the sun rose on a new day, I knew that the night of the full moon would always be a special memory for me and my ancestors. It was a night that had tested our strength and courage, and one that had brought us closer together.

As I walked through the streets of the small town, I couldn't shake the feeling of unease that had settled over me. It had been a week since the ritual, and strange things had been happening ever since.

At first, it had just been small things - objects moving on their own, strange noises in the night. But as the days passed, the occurrences became more and more intense.

I knew that it had to be connected to the ritual we had performed, but I had no idea how to stop it. I had consulted with a local spiritualist, but even they had been unable to provide any answers.

It was a dark and stormy night, and as I walked home from work, I couldn't help but feel like I was being watched. I quickened my pace, desperate to get home and lock the door behind me.

But as I reached my front door, I was confronted by a figure shrouded in darkness. It reached out towards me, and I let out a scream as I felt myself being pulled into the darkness.

When I came to, I was lying on the ground outside my house, the storm raging around me. I had no memory of what had happened, but I knew that I had to find a way to reverse the effects of the ritual before it was too late.

With the help of my ancestors and the spirits we had invoked, I set out on a journey to discover the truth and restore balance to the land. It was a long and dangerous journey, but in the end, we were able to reverse the effects

THE SELECTION OF A SACRED STRAWBERRY

of the ritual and return things to normal.

As the sun rose on a new day, I knew that the night of the ritual would always be a memory that stayed with me. It had tested my strength and courage, and had shown me the true power of the spirits.

As I sat in my living room, surrounded by the remnants of the ritual, I couldn't help but feel a sense of awe and respect for the traditions of my ancestors. The night of the ritual had been a true test of strength and courage and had shown me the true power of rituals.

I had always been skeptical of the old ways, but now I knew that there was something special about them. They connected us to our ancestors and to the spirits that surrounded us and gave us a way to tap into a power that was beyond our understanding.

But I also knew that with great power came great responsibility. The night of the ritual had shown me that we had to be careful with the rituals we performed, and make sure that we were using them for the right reasons.

As I gathered up the ritual items and prepared to put them away, I knew that the experience would stay with me for the rest of my life. It had shown me the importance of tradition and the power of rituals and brought me closer to my ancestors and the spirits that surrounded us.

I was grateful for the experience and knew that it would always be a special memory for me. The night of the ritual had truly been a life-changing experience and one that I would never forget.

CHAPTER TWENTY-THREE
THE PEEPAL TREE TEMPLE

By Gitanjali Maria

Palayapura was a sleepy little town, nestled at the foothills of the Western Ghats. It was known for its cardamom and pepper cultivation. And of late, it's zeal to send its youngsters abroad for education and jobs.

Muthukumar aka Muthu's house was one of the many tiny houses made of bamboo, hay, and cement that dotted the sloppy terrains of this sleepy village. Muthu was going to the visa office in Madras (Chennai) today for completing the paperwork to go to the US to do his post-graduation in engineering (MS). He had already got admission to a prestigious university there with a scholarship grant.

"Take this prasad, son", his mother shouted as he began leaving to go to the railway station to catch the train to Madras.

His mother came hurrying, bringing a plate with a small statue of Lord Ganesh, a burning lamp, some milk sweets, and powder to draw tilak on the forehead.

She made three circles in the air with the plate around his head, before applying the tilak on his forehead, and putting a piece of the milk sweet into his mouth.

"All for good luck", she said smiling at his exasperated look. "The Gods will help you get the visa soon."

"I'm late amma, let me go", Muthu said before his mother could add more rituals to bring him luck.

He hurried to the auto rickshaw stand to get a rickshaw to the station. The way to the auto rickshaw stand was a five minute walk past the old government school where he had studied for fourteen long years. Just before the school stood a huge, old peepal tree.

As he was crossing it, he remembered how during his SSLC exam (10th class), he had circled three times around the tree for good luck and had scored a whopping 95%, bringing him in among the top ten in the state. And another time, circling the tree had helped him crack the exams for admission to the engineering college in the city.

Why not do it again? Isn't this an equally important event?

With his heavy shoulder bag, he quickly half-ran and half-walked around the peepal tree. As he was completing the circle and proceeding to catch the auto rickshaw, a voice from behind called out leisurely, "Muthu, where are you off to?"

Muthu turned back to look. It was his friend Vikas, actually a good-for-nothing fellow. "I'm going to Madras for some work." Revealing the exact nature of work may result in it not being successful, something else he'd come to believe over time. The lad's evil eye might cast a spell and make him not get what he wants. So, he said nothing more and hurried off. "But why to circumambulate this old tree thrice?" Vikas wondered aloud.

Oh, he saw it. I only hope he keeps his mouth shut, Muthu muttered under his breath as he walked faster away from Vikas.

Three weeks later, the whole village was euphoric. Muthu was finally going to America. His visa had come through, the ticket was ready, and all he needed was to reach the airport at the midnight for his early morning flight.

Everyone clambered around his house, wishing him luck and enquiring about the processes he had followed. Though some of the people from the village had gone to the Middle East for petty jobs, he was the first one to go to the dream land, America.

"It was God's will and my prayers", his mother said, turning toward the many miniature and large images of gods and goddesses kept in the pooja room and touching her hands to her eyes in reverence. "I even offered malar naivedyam to Lord Krishna for this", she said.

"It was written in his horoscope. I only made it when he was small", the temple priest chimed in.

"I saw him circumambulating the peepal tree before going to Madras. That brought him luck", Vikas announced to no one in particular in the group.

But everyone suddenly went quiet, each wondering what external elements were either helping or impeding their growth.

As the clock inched towards seven 'o'clock, and the light started fading and the stars came out, some of those gathered started going back to their homes after bidding Muthu further luck. "Best of luck".

A few others, mostly men, stayed back, ready to travel the four-and-a-half-hour journey to the airport at Cochin to bid their star kid a safe and happy journey.

THE SELECTION OF A SACRED STRAWBERRY

Almost six months after Muthu landed on the shores of America, another lad from the village was trying his luck for going overseas. "It's so tough to get admissions. And then there's the visa procedure where they ask difficult questions in their heavy accents", he lamented to Vikas.

Vikas nodded in acknowledgment even though he had no experience of these. He had never been interested in studies or in going abroad. Many in the village believed that his growth had stunted after he met with an accident when he was eleven, damaging his brain. "The Gods will take care of you", his parents and relatives had said to him then and over and over again as the years passed by, and he seemed to believe in it in earnest, never putting in hard work or having ambitions.

After some silence, he said, "Maybe you should go and circumambulate the peepal tree thrice. That's what Muthu did to get his visa."

"But what use is that? Is it some belief? Or some ritual before someone tries to go overseas?"

"I don't know about it. But what harm is there in trying? It will hardly take a minute. Do it whenever you pass by there and it will surely help you get admission and a visa."

Four weeks later an elated Raju told Vikas, "Hey! I just received the letter for a doctorate at the New South Wales University in Australia. I had hoped to go to America like Muthu, but I hear Australia is better. Finally, the gods have heard my prayer!"

"All thanks to the peepal tree!" Vikas replied drily.

"True. It was only yesterday that I did the circumambulation ritual. I had lost all hope of going abroad."

Soon, news spread wide about the peepal tree and the ritual of circumambulating it to get the visa to go abroad.

The young men of the village who wished to go abroad, be it to the Middle East or further west circumambulated the tree thrice before going for their interviews and appointments. One of them put a vermillion mark on the tree as a sign of prayer while another one tied a sacred scarf around it. Some of them also left tiny idols of the lords under the tree and did pooja there.

"We must build a temple around the tree. It has helped lots of our youth to prosper", the village headman announced one day as the village gathered for the annual meeting.

"That is the right thing to do", everyone echoed

The villagers pooled money to build a small temple near the tree. It came to be known as the VISA temple, for the exclusive prayers that priests there offered to help devotees get their tickets to go abroad. Circumambulating the old peepal tree was definitely one of the rituals in the many that the priests subscribed to ensure a smooth visa process.

Soon the fame of the visa temple spread and people from far and wide came to sleepy Palayapura to pray for their successful passage abroad, to greener pastures.

When Muthu returned five years later, he was amazed to see the way his village had changed.

There were a lot more restaurants, many started by acquaintances and friends. One group of his school friends had started 'The Visa Temple Restaurant & Hotel' while a rival gang had started the hotel 'The Passage Abroad' just a few meters away.

As he stepped down from the rickety government bus that still serviced the village and brought him home from the airport, he was surprised at the way the staff at the two hotels tried to lure him.

It wasn't until Vikas saw him and pulled him away from their clutches that he was able to breathe freely.

"Palayapura is famous now!" he said, and added cheekily "All thanks to you!"

"How?"

Over the conversation that ensued as they walked to his house, punctured multiple times by acquaintances who stopped to greet him and make enquires, he learned how the act of circumambulating the peepal tree had become the hope of thousands for a passage out of the country.

As they passed the temple, he saw the long line of devotees who had reached there early morning. Some were walking around the tree, some rolled on the ground around the tree (angapradashinam), while others waited before the temple door to glance at the deities and take the prasad from the priest.

"Not just visas, people also to pray for their children to study well, get good marks, and marry educated partners."

Could it be really true? Muthu wondered. Many years ago he had walked around the tree, praying for easy questions in the exams and good marks, and had got them. Was it just a coincidence or did the peepal tree really bring good luck?

He looked harder at the tree, a sense of divine notion rising in him. He'd never given the tree a second thought even when circumambulating it. He'd just done it by instinct, merging what he thought were separate rituals - worshipping the sacred tree and circumambulating a holy thing. He had never thought it would yield such divine results for hundreds of people.

His mother waited for him at their doorstep with the traditional lamp and the plate of prasad. She had added a few more grey hairs and wrinkles than the last time he saw her.

As soon as she had finished with her rituals of welcoming him and warding off evil eyes, he asked about her health, and then about the temple near the peepal tree.

"Yes, you should go there and do the prayers and rituals before going back. Good that you saw it for yourself, the long line of people who believe and pray there."

"But amma, I've been doing that all along. I have circumambulated the old peepal tree many times in my life. Before exams, after exams, before interviews. But I never thought there was any big deal it that. It was just a gesture of luck... "

His mother's stern look silenced his rant.

"Good you have been praying at the peepal tree temple for long. Just continue it."

"And luck is nothing but God's grace. Remember that", she added.

"And don't call that peepal tree old. Old is gold ", she said rather angrily. He hugged her lovingly.

Muthu went each day to the peepal tree temple or the Visa temple as they called it colloquially to just observe the happenings. There were sometimes massive demonstrations of emotions – chest-beating, hair-pulling, and tears. At other times, it was quiet, the tension and anxiety that the devotees felt vibrated in the air. All of it for educational or professional achievement.

His rational brain couldn't accept it. It was his hard work, burning the midnight oil that had got him so far, that's what he had said to everyone all along.

But as the date for his visa renewal interview drew closer, he couldn't but let his legs take him to the queue of aspirant devotees.

He found himself taking the banana leaf with prasad from the priest and circumambulating the peepal tree, his old friend.

And in three days his passport had arrived with the visa stamp, the renewal process having gone smoothly.

"See, I told you, disbeliever! All that you need to do to get your visa is to go to the temple", both Vikas and his mother chided him.

He wanted to argue that it was his documents and good conduct in the US and during the interview that helped him get the visa and all other success, but he then remembered that he had gone and stood in the queue, willingly and consciously.

Rituals simply complement whatever effort one puts in, he concluded. No harm in it unless it hurts someone else.

His mother seemed to read his thoughts, and they smiled.

Glossary:

- Prasad – A devotional offering made to gods, typically consisting of food that is later given to devotees.
- Tilak - A sacred mark made on the forehead
- Amma – Mother
- Pooja – Prayer
- Malar naivedyam – A special prayer and prasad

CHAPTER TWENTY-FOUR

MY CONFESSION

By Ninad Bhangle

During my childhood, I wanted to die saving someone's life. As I grew up, I realized it is not worth it. Sacrifice is the biggest lie sold in this world. Nothing glorious about it. Absolutely nothing.

As I grew up, I realized, it is better to kill. Because there are quite a lot of people in this world who deserve to die. And they will, as long as I am alive!

I am not a killer. I am a vigilante. It is my duty to kill – for the righteous good! I have killed 27 so far, but my list is long. You may be in my list. So beware.

Let me tell you all why I kill and how. Just to give you a flavor of what goes into this gorgeous mind of mine. You should be inspired by my story. It is worth it. So read on!

I was born in a simple middle-class, God-fearing household in Kolhapur, a small town in Maharashtra. I lived with my parents and my grandparents – a typical, Indian joint family. Or so I thought!

I was just five when I witnessed my parents kicking my grandparents out of the home. The bitter feuds for property, the fights over petty issues had finally reached its zenith when they decided to take the dreaded step. My grandparents were sent to an old-age home in Kolhapur and left to die. And then they did die, within a span of six months. First my Aaba (grandfather), and then a few days later, my Aaji (grandmother).

Ever since they left our home, I lost the will to live there. I was very close to my grandparents. I loved hearing stories about their youth, their experiences. My grandparents weren't very educated but they were avid readers. While my Aaba taught me mathematics tables, my Aaji educated me about stars and myriad constellations. I was mesmerized by my grandparents and loved spending every waking moment with them, much more than with my parents.

After their death, I decided – I need to toughen up. And so I did. For seven years, I trained in martial arts. Karate and taekwondo both. My mission was clear – to avenge the death of my grandparents.

On my thirteenth birthday, also coincidentally my grandfather's eightieth birthday, I decided – today is the moment. When my parents were asleep, I walked into their room. I gently woke my father up. He looked at me lovingly, and I stabbed him. First the eyes, then chest. He shouted in shock as I kept stabbing him, violently until he had no voice, no breath.

But, the job was only half done. My mother who was in deep sleep thanks to her sleeping pills prescribed by her therapist needed to be punished. I slapped her on both cheeks to wake her from her slumber. I smiled and said, "It's time to go." I stabbed her twice in the chest, slit her neck and let the blood drain from her body and the colour from her face.

Satisfied, I took a bath, changed into a fresh pair of clothes, stole some money and ran away from home. Forever. Where can a thirteen year old find shelter? I took the train to Mumbai – a city with over 2.1 crore population, where I can hide easily and start afresh.

I started working at a small shop in Dadar, near Siddhivinayak temple selling tea and vada pav, the staple food of Mumbai. Everyone lovingly called me "Chotu" (slang for Kid). If only they knew the "grand feats" that, this Chotu had done just a week before. But I chose to remain silent, gulped my ego and went along with my mundane life.

A part of me was worried that I would be caught, but nobody really cares about a middle class family's death. I was very sure my parents' murder would have gone unnoticed. Though I hoped at least someone would have taken the pains of lighting their pyre; else, their bodies would be stinking by now.

I started staying in a small hut at Sewri, but I was enchanted by the grandeur of the city of Mumbai – the city of dreams as they say. Once I was walking around Dadar West, the beautiful Siddhivinayak temple, the skyscrapers of Prabhadevi and that is when I noticed, "Maitri – An old age home". Maitri literally translates to companionship. I looked inside and noticed more than 50 senior citizens inside, mostly walking with crutches, a few on wheelchair, abandoned by their families, living their last few years in the nondescript shelter home.

I was furious. How dare people leave their own parents out to die? My mind went back to my dear grandparents who were also kicked out of our home. I decided – I needed to teach these ungrateful sons, daughters and grandchildren a lesson.

I took up odd cleaning jobs at the shelter home. It gave me a chance to interact with the elderly, take care of them, bond with them and immerse myself in their stories. In them, I found glimpses of my grandparents.

But I had an ulterior motive. My main reason behind working at Maitri was to scout my next target. Every week, at least three new oldies were inducted into the shelter home. Often, it would be a son or daughter promising they are keeping their parents temporarily, only for a few days and they will soon be back. Bloody liars! They never came – none of them, while the oldies kept waiting. So naïve.

My first target were Mr. and Mrs. Kulkarni, staying in a plush apartment complex in Worli. Strange that people could be so rich yet they cannot take care of their own parents. For a week, I stalked them, understanding their daily routine. Both husband and wife loved jogging at Shivaji Park and often ended their run with a glass of watermelon juice. That was my chance. I befriended the juice seller and started working there. One fine day, I slipped in rat poison in the juice. It took 6-8 hours for the poison to take action and then they passed away due to internal organ failures. Smooth and suave. I was quite proud of myself.

A few weeks later, I found my next target. Ibrahim Khan. A CA by profession, he had come with his mother to drop his paternal grandfather. Apparently, Ibrahim's father had passed away last year and both he and his mother were too engrossed in their lives to take care of the dead man's father. And Maitri was their way out. I befriended Mansoor Khan, a 74-year-old retired mathematics teacher by profession. Hearing his stories in the shelter home over the next week became my pastime. Mansoor Chacha reminded me of my grandfather; that is when I decided,

Ibrahim needed to be taught a lesson.

I chose the perfect time – Makar Sankranti. Ibrahim and his friends were participating in a kite-flying competition at Shivaji Park, barely 500 meters from his apartment complex. I decided to become one of the 'manjha' (string) sellers at the venue. Ibrahim was adept at kite flying and taking down his opponent's kites. After the event, Ibrahim and his friends downed a few vodka shots in the back seat of his car, parked in a desolate spot slightly away from the venue. I waited for the right opportunity for him to be alone. When his mother called, he stepped away to speak with her. I followed him gently, with a string in hand and deliberately bumped into him and his phone fell on the ground. He looked into my eyes with disgust and bent forward to pick it up. In one swift movement, I used the manjha to slit his neck. Just to be extra sure, I stabbed his chest with my pocketknife and walked away from there, without turning back. Next day, I was apprised of his death by Mansoor Chacha at Maitri. He felt genuinely sad but said that it was god's will and he had accepted it.

Wow, I felt like God. I felt I could control people's destiny. Soon, killing became a ritual.

Every few weeks, I found a new victim. My modus operandi was fairly simple – track the victim for a week to understand their patterns, use a murder weapon that is easily accessible and then finish off the victim with alacrity and dexterity.

As I said earlier, my current count stands at 27. Not bad for 6 months of effort! But I also know that considering the rate at which old age homes are being constructed, many with 100% occupancy, I realized that the journey has just begun.

Do you still think I am a killer? Or do you agree that I am doing a noble service – cleansing the dirt of people. My ritual was cleansing the city of filthy people – my decisive contribution towards "shuddikaran" (purification)

Sometimes I wonder, how can people abandon their parents easily? I feel appalled that once a person crosses the age of 70, they suddenly become a liability.

Sometimes I wonder, aren't there enough nurses or caregivers available who can take care of the old ones? Can't the children afford care for their parents? People spend insane amounts on materialistic gifts and vacations and expensive status symbols, yet when it comes to our elders, we, as a society, seem to have become emotionless.

I do not intend to be preachy – this has strengthened my resolve to continue on my path until I cleanse the society of this evil. Every morning, I will find a new victim. That's my resolution. I will make killing my tapasya (my penance).

You must be wondering, why am I making this confession? That too in a national publication. Why do I want to reveal my identity? You must be wondering, is it to warn you? Or am I so pompous in believing that I will not ever be caught?

I have just one word response: BEWARE! Beware if you are one of those who don't take care of their parents. Beware if you are even thinking about abandoning them. Beware if you are engaging in fraudulent court cases to deprive the elderly of love, respect and their rights. Beware if you are impure. Because, then my ritual of shuddikaran will find its way towards you!

Now, if you are a cop and search for me, I would be happy to surrender. But only if you promise to protect all its citizens – not just from external threats but from the more pertinent internal threats, threats within the family.

You take an oath to protect the vulnerable, then why is it that you cannot stop this injustice?

If you are a lawmaker, why don't we have strong laws in our country protecting the rights of the elderly? If you are human rights activists, why are you blind towards their pain? WHY?

Anyway, I do not intend my confession to be a rant. I understand the shortcomings of the system and the society, which is why I will continue down my path. My ritual will go on – until I am alive. And this is a promise to my Aaji and Aaba and every other grandparents who suffer each day.

I have a database of over 180 old-age homes across Mumbai, with more than 17000 residents, 70 percent of which are cases of abandonment. Quite a large sample size to keep me busy at least for the next two years. Maybe I should build an army of like-minded souls who can join me in my rituals. This will enable me to expand my operations across the country. Over time, I can build a new religion – if not a religion, at least a cult. Long way to go! I am quite ambitious and excited!

Before I wrap up this letter, in case you are wondering, Maitri does not exist. I just used a random fictitious name. Same goes for Mr. and Mrs. Kulkarni. Even Mr. Khan.

Secondly, I may be anywhere, in any part of the city, tracking any old-age home, stalking anyone of you right now. And you wouldn't even know. After all, in a city of 2.1 crore population, in a city that never sleeps, I am just another teenager. Or well, I could be lying about my age too!

Signing off,

Mr. X (well, it could be Ms. too!)

CHAPTER TWENTY-FIVE

THE MIDNIGHT RITUAL

By Adyasha Acharya

The sky is a light shade of saffron as I stare at it from the roof of a twenty-five-storeyed building. When you are a supernatural being with two wings, the sky becomes your home. The moon, the stars, and the sun your friends.

"Twilight with you, just perfect," a deep velvety voice shifts my attention away from the creation of God.

Mikhail smiles at me, leaning against the door leading to the staircase. His sandy hair is wind-blown and his blue eyes capture mine with the intensity of an ocean.

"You are early," I say turning back towards the sky as he joins me.

"I couldn't wait for midnight," he replies casually. Tonight is the night of the ritual. All the warrior angels inhabiting earth gather in Alaska under the veil of the Northern Lights to celebrate the last day of the year. It is the one time of the year we all get to see each other, when I get to meet my brother and father even.

Mikhail and I however being mates, see each other every day. We are the only angels who reside here in Alaska.

I nudge his shoulder. "What has got you so excited this time?"

Last year, on this day we were battling demons and weren't even sure if we would ever see each other again. This time, I sincerely pray that nothing bad happens.

"Well, we shall be announcing to everyone that we are getting married." He grins and I smile. Before we had met, Mikhail was known as one of the greatest warriors of our angelic history. He still is but he is no more that cold assassin he was.

"That is worth the excitement. My brother will kill us both though since we haven't told him about our engagement."

He huffs. "I really don't care about what Harvey thinks. He is your elder brother but acts like the younger one." I narrow my eyes. "You know it too, love."

We stay there talking till the stars come out like bright diamonds in the sky.

A loud flap of wings catches our attention. Mikhail tenses and reveals his huge raven black wings which cover almost the whole of the terrace. I relax when I see the outline of the angel's face.

"Dana," my brother greets wrapping me in a big hug. Harvey isn't like other warrior angels. He is light-hearted and a happy-go-lucky kind of celestial. Not usually the type of your resident angel. "Mikhail."

"We weren't expecting you until a few hours," Mikhail says drawing back his wings. I still remember our last battle with the demons where he almost lost one of his wings to save me. I can never repay him ever for that and it is why I have sworn to stand by his side the rest of my life.

"I wouldn't have come this early either had I not got the news from Dad." He frowns which tells me the news isn't good. And if a thing has worried Harvey that means it is a definite matter of concern.

Alcaeus, our father is a millennia year old angel, a member of the High Council. The High Council is a body of warrior angels who oversee the functions we do. They provide us with our assignment. They decide the rewards and the punishment. And they are not really friendly.

Our father however, changed after our mother died a decade ago in a battle. Ever since, he has become more attentive towards us. And even after a decade I sometimes can't believe that.

"What is it?" I ask then stop myself. This place is not the right one to talk about something so important. "We should go home and talk."

Mikhail nods, his face grave. "I agree with Dana."

All the three of us open our wings, mine white, my brother's light grey like my father's. Mikhail and I lead our brother to our house on the outskirts of the city. It is large cottage with three rooms, a kitchen, living room and a huge garden.

We decided this location because of the scenic beauty. The Northern lights cover the sky over us and it is the most beautiful sight I have ever seen. It is like our home in Heaven.

I land first while Mikhail does a perimeter sweep and joins both of us inside a minute later. "Nice house," Harvey compliments glancing around.

"Thanks. Do you want a cup of coffee or hot chocolate?"

He grins at me at the mention of his favourite drink. "I could never pass on a cup of hot chocolate."

My soulmate joins me on the kitchen counter while my brother takes a seat on the couch in the living room. "What do you think it is?" Mikhail whispers to me.

"I don't know. Dad didn't try to reach out to me." I take out three mugs and clean them. "Your brother tell you anything?"

Mikhail's younger brother and his wife, Zanver and Selena reside in Russia where the High Council has a headquarters. It is the only place on earth where they have their own building. "I didn't receive any message from him. Except that they shall be joining us tonight."

"Well let's hope it isn't demons anymore," I mumble as I follow him back to the living room.

Harvey is staring at the wall when I place a mug in front of him. "Thanks, sis." He suddenly grabs my hand catching me off-guard. "Is that a ring?" I nod smiling. "You got engaged and you didn't tell me?"

"We were going to tell you tonight," I say feeling guilty. "It has only been a few weeks. And I thought I should tell you this face to face and not on phone."

"Congratulations!" He pats me shoulder and salutes at Mikhail. "I know you'll keep her happy."

Mikhail arches a brow. "Shouldn't you be warning me or something?"

"Nah, that would be fake anyway."

I roll my eyes while Mikhail shakes his head. We both sit down on the sofa opposite to my brother. "Okay, now spill." I have a very thin line of patience when it comes to secrets and 'I am here to tell you something' kind of things.

"The High Council is getting re-elected."

I blink twice doubting if I heard him right. Getting re-elected? The High Council of Warrior angels. Is this a joke or something?

"You serious?" Mikhail asks reading my thoughts. This is one of the abilities we share as soulmates. "They have been the same since time immemorial. What in heavens happened?"

He is right indeed. The High Council including our father includes a bunch of orthodox angels who are as old as time itself. Why would they suddenly decide this?

"Yes." Harvey places his mug on the tea-table. "After what happened with demons last year, Father said there was a clash of thoughts among the Council members. Mikhail's father and ours and a few of our other friends they thought it was time they retired and gave their positions to a new generation."

Mikhail runs his hand through his golden hair. "I agree with them." I spare him a glance. "Dana, love, the Council is a bunch of useless, power-craving fools. Including my father and yours." Mikhail has always hated the Council for their ways. And he hated them even more when the Council forced me to sacrifice myself last year to save themselves. They also wanted me to let Mikhail die after he tried to save me. I used my healing ability against their wishes to save him. And I would do it a thousand times again for him.

"So, what do we do now?" Harvey asks.

"We wait two more hours," I say glancing at the wall clock.

The two hours are spent in brainstorming who might be elected into the new High Council. I don't have a clue as to who my father might choose. Mikhail says he barely knows how his father's mind operates and he doesn't want to guess.

The three of us take off around fifteen minutes to midnight to the spot. It is a clearing in the woods. Since we spend all our days here, it is easy for us to find it.

Dad is already waiting for us while a few other angels are busy lighting the bonfire. Others like Mikhail's father are busy chatting near the frozen lake. Food and elixir are being served at the far end.

"Dad," I greet him formally. Embracing him in front of the High Council seems inappropriate while he has that cold unfriendly image.

"Daughter." He nods at Harvey. "Son."

"Everyone please gather around the bonfire," Aldine, a member of the High Council announces. The other members including Dad and Mikhail's father walk to the other side of the huge flames.

Mikhail comes to stand near me his arm brushing mine.

"Before we start our ritual, the High Council has to make an announcement," Dad says his features grim. "This wasn't a decision on which everyone agreed to but it was high time we did this. We have decided to elect new members to the High Council."

A hush falls through the crowd. They weren't expecting this. Not tonight. Not ever.

"It is a big step," Mikhail's father, Caviar sounds uninterested. I haven't had many interactions with him but he didn't sound so thrilled when I told him about his son and me being mates. He said mates are just distractions. I never talked to him after that. As for Mikhail, he has never liked his father.

"Who are the new members?" someone from the crowd asks.

"I didn't think we would be coming to this," Zanver's voice surprises me. Mikhail claps his brother on the back. Selena gives me a quick hug. "Father didn't tell us anything about this."

"Father never tells us anything," Mikhail corrects him.

Aldine takes the lead again. "We haven't yet decided the full council but we are first welcoming two warriors to join us. They have proven themselves time and again that they are worthy of this position. Dana, daughter of Alcaeus and Mikhail, son of Caviar, we welcome you to the High Council of Warrior angels."

I glance at Mikhail in astonishment. His ocean blue eyes stare back at me with surprise. We both weren't expecting this.

Harvey starts clapping first followed by Zanver and his wife. "You both earned it," Mikhail's younger brother grins at us.

"What do you say?" Mikhail asks me. I can hear a hint of excitement in his voice.

It will be a difficult path but we are in this together. "We do this together."

Dad gives me an appreciative nod. "Midnight has arrived, angels." His voice echoes through the clearing. "We are here together to celebrate our wins against the evil, to the warriors we lost and to the alliances we've gained."

The crowd echoes my father's words. We join in raising our voices.

"We have to make an announcement," Mikhail announces once the voices have died down. "Dana and I are getting married and we want all those present here to be a part of our happiness."

"And we want you all to give us your blessings," I add. "I know Mikhail and I aren't as experienced as the current council members but we will try our best to carry out this responsibility. We just expect your trust and cooperation in return." I let my wings free and soar high up. Mikhail joins me a moment later.

One by one all the angels join us in the night sky. We circle the fire. It is a part of the ritual.

"The year is about to end," Mikhail's father says. "We conclude our ritual by sharing one last thought of this year with our closed one."

Mikhail looks at me and motions for me to follow him. We both fly to where the enchanting green lights in the sky take us.

"You know I always thought Alaska would be where we would settle in," he says taking my hand. "But now it seems we would be going to Russia."

"Do you think we did the right thing by accepting?"

His smile lights up his whole face. "I think this is fate."

I smile back at him. "I think it is destiny."

CHAPTER TWENTY-SIX

The Lighthouse Keeper

By Will Sandkvist

Dark waves crashed against the rocks, scattering whipped seafoam across the beach stretching far. Fine sand like ash under the dim light of a shy moon hiding behind clouds. Tiny fragments of smooth sea glass gleamed among the dullness as a flickering brightness caught the right angles.

"Who can sail without wind?" Echoing between the stone walls of an old lighthouse, a voice could be heard. A sad haunting suspended in the cold air. A broken record, the catching on bumps and scratches. A ritual just as much as a prayer. "Who can row without oars?"

The owner of the voice, a woman with silvery white hair, strands wavy, her loose-fitted dress shirt bleached by sea salt, moved around the room with ease. Pearls of water dripped down the glass windows. Decaying floorboards creaked under her booths. "Who can leave a parting friend, without shedding tears?"

The lihthouse keeper approached a chest of drawers, intricately decorated with golden flora pulling the attention away from the signs of wear and tear. The hinges groaned under the strain of being moved- the wood had already settled comfortably in its position. With the exhaustion of power, the muscles tensing under almost translucent skin, the top drawer revealed enough of its insides for her to stick her hands inside and fish out a small silver coffer. The shine dulled down from being tucked away for years, waiting for its purpose to arrive. And now it had.

Carved into the smooth metal was a name - Thomas Lee - spelled out in cursive, salt crystals forming in the groves of the title. And under it a date -1891-1964 - carved with equal care.

" I can sail without the wind." The deeper rasping of a voice used to being alone dipped in and out from the whistling of the storm outside. Shrinking seagulls in the distance unknowingly adding to the song.

A thin chain was lifted from its nest under the fabric of her shirt revealing a key, still warm from where its polished surface had rested against her sternum. Clicking into place within the coffer's lock, a soft pop could be heard as the top came undone.

Empty.

The inside was clad in crushed velvet, the color like a starless sky; a black hole ready to swallow whatever was placed inside.

"I can row without oars."

A cough.

A slender neck stretched backward exposing the jugular. Her fingers glided along the curve, fingertips barely touching as they followed the pace of something moving beneath flesh and blood. Slowly making its way up her throat and finally to her parting lips where, upon her tongue, an iridescent pearl had appeared. She took the pearl between her fingers and held it up to the window where it scattered the moonbeam shining through like a suncatcher before placing it in its new home inside the coffer.

"But I can't leave a parting friend, without shedding tears." As the song died on her lips the top of the silver box was clicked shut, its internal mechanics working the lock, sealing the pearl away from the salty dampness hanging heavy in the air. The coffer was placed back inside the top drawer. The lightkeeper pressed her hip into the wood, ready to use it as extra leverage to trust the heavy furniture shut when–

Cling...

The sound of bells clinking together.

The ritual, without malice for being disturbed, was left unfinished as the woman moved over to the window. Using the back of her hand to wipe away the condensation from the glass and looking down on the outstretched beach below and upon the shadow anxiously moving across it. Disturbing the fine sand. Dark hair dancing in the wind and obscuring the face from view.

Scratched leather boots, discolored from being exposed to decades of usage of whale oil, moved quickly down the spiraling staircase of chipped, slippery stone steps. Snatching a lantern from its hinges as she lands on the first floor, inhaling a deep breath before braving the storm outside.

"Mikael, where are you?" A frightened cry cut through the fog. Bare feet slipping on slick stones. The billowing of a skirt whipping around bruised legs.

The lightkeeper silently approached her, her own feet steady on the uneven ground, the beach seemingly paving a safe path for her to walk. "You won't find who you are seeking. I'm afraid you and I are the only ones here." She presented an outstretched hand for comfort. "May I ask for your name?"

The distressed young lady turned around to face the lighthouse keeper, her cheeks streaked with tears, eyelashes heavy and clumped together. "No, you don't understand. He told me he would meet me there."

"Meet you where?"

"The garden. He told me we could live in the garden forever. That, once inside its gates, no one would be able to keep us apart."

The lightkeeper tried again, leaving her hand open. "My name is Dawn. You're Melina Jones, right?"

Confusion filled Melina at the mention of her name. She stopped her movements to look at the lightkeeper, really look at her. Noticing how her hair lay relaxed over her shoulders, how her exposed skin was free of goosebumps, unaffected by the harsh winds, unlike her own that was shivering in the cold. She looked around at the scenery surrounding them. The waves crashing up against the rocky cliff sides. The almost black sand beneath their feet. The full moon, ever so round, giant in the night sky arranged with the clearest constellation she's ever seen. And it was as if it finally dawned on her. "He's not coming, is he?" A single tear fell down her face and clung to her cheekbone.

Dawn, accepting her hand wasn't wanted, straightened up. "I can't answer that. He might still have time, or perhaps he has already passed and is waiting for you on the other side. more than that I can not tell you. You need to find those answers on your own."

"What do you mean ´passed on´? He was right there. He was- are you telling me you killed him? That you killed...me?" Anger flared up from the embers left by the confusion.

"I am not here to harm you, Melina. I am simply here to guide you to the other side." She made a second attempt to reach out, this time to put her hand on Melina's shoulder.

"I'm not dead!" Melina shrugged her hand off, backing away. "This is all a cruel dream. When I wake up, Mikael will be there and this will be nothing but a bad memory." She turned to leave. Walked away along the shoreline when Dawn's hand enclasped her wrist.

"Once you reach the beach you only really have one choice. You can't leave, not the same anyway. I think you already know that."

"Watch me."

"Melina–"

Smack.

The metal lantern Dawn had brought from the lighthouse fell to the ground with a soft thump. Her fingers graced the blooming bruise where Melina's hand had struck her cheek. She looked expressionless at her hand as if to inspect any evidence of possible injury, but found her delicate hand clean.

Melina, the hem of her dress soaked from backing a bit too far out, seawater chilling her ankles, sunk to her knees. She was weeping open and loud. Wiping her face with the sleeves of her blouse like a child. "I just want to see him again. Even for just one more glance."

The lightkeeper approached her, now with the same precaution one would while approaching a cornered animal. She didn't extend her hand or offer comfort. Instead, she too fell to her knees in the sand. Eyes waiting for contact.

"You spoke of a garden. Can you tell me more about it?"

Melina didn't meet her eyes, instead furiously rubbing at her eyes. "Why? Why does it even matter?"

"Humour me." The beginning of a smile tugged at the corners of her lips.

Melina gave up on scrubbing her face, letting her arms fall heavy in her lap. She drew in a wet breath. "The garden is filled with gorgeous roses, tall bushes with the brightest leaves, but with no thorns to prick your fingers on. Cracked cobblestone paths where nature has taken over. And in the middle is an intricately built wooden pavilion with vines climbing up its beams and reaching across its roof. "

"It sounds beautiful."

"It is. Or so I've been told." She picked up a black stone buried in the sand, turning it over and over in her hand, fidgeting with it. Her ribcage expanded and fell slowly, the motion barely visible. Sniffling, she finally looked up at Dawn, her glossy ones finding her patient ones. "So this is it then? No turning back or do-over?"

"I´m sorry."

Melina weighted the stone in her palm, turning it over one last time, and skipped it across the surface of the water where it bounced a few times before sinking to the bottom. "It's alright. I think I'm ready now."

Dawn stood up, helping Melina to her feet. With the two women facing each other, Melina with her back facing the rough sea, Dawn placed her hands on either side of Melina's face. "When you close your eyes, I want you to picture your garden. The roses, the cobblestones, and the pavilion." Instead of flinching away, Melisa relaxed into the lightkeeper's touch. "Keep their vivid image in your mind as you step into the other side and they will guide you to where you need to be." Dawn leaned in, closing the gap between them, and kissed her. Heavy eyelids fell shut. Dark hair, despite the winds, stilled and wrapped around her shoulders. Fingers relaxed by her sides.

Dawn swallowed and let go of Melina, her now compliant body turned around towards the wide open water. The waves were calmer, not hitting the cliffs quite as harshly.

"Goodbye, Melina Jones. May your journey be kind."

Without giving an answer, or opening her eyes, Melina walked into the sea, her skirt floating out around her like the pad of a water lily, the fabric growing darker and heavier with each step. As the water reached her chest, her body turned into sea foam and was carried away by the waves.

The lightkeeper picked up the discarded lantern from the sand and walked back to the lighthouse-a tall shadow in the background. Crying seagulls circled the building before finding a place to perch.

Boots made their way up the spiraling stairs. Clattering of stone and metal as the lantern was placed back in its hold on the wall. "Who can sail without wind?" She sang, wiping away a light trickling of blood coming out of her nose.

Once back on the top floor the lightkeeper approached the waiting chest of drawers, standing with its top drawer open just as she had left it. "Who can row without oars?" And the ritual began all over from where the previous one had been interrupted. "Who can leave a parting friend, without shedding tears?"

From inside the drawer, which had previously been empty except for the decorated coffer, she pulled another one out. Delicate filigree spread across the lid and wrapped over the sides, and just like the previous one this one too was engraved with a name - Melina Jones - and under it a date - 1940-1964.

"I can sail without the wind." She fished out the key from under her shirt. Inserted it into the lock and opened the lid. "I can row without oars."

Leaning her head back, using her fingers to ease the motion, she brought the pearl back up and held it in her hands. A perfectly round pearl with a slight green tint to it, not quite achieving its iridescent shine yet- she had been too young for that.

Dawn placed the pearl in its coffer. Closed the lid to the sound of the lock clicking in place. "But I can't leave a parting friend..." She lowered the coffer back into the drawer. Lining her hip up against the drawer, a hand resting on the top for extra leverage, she pushed the heavy furniture shut with a heavy groan of wood and metal boxes clinking together. "...Without shedding tears."

Cling. Cling. Cling.

CHAPTER TWENTY-SEVEN

THE SACRIFICE BEARER

By Oluwatoyin Magbagbeola

Destiny is the one chosen by the Oracle to be the next sacrifice bearer for the upcoming ritual of the Osun/Osogbo festival which is done every year in a little town of Osogbo, Nigeria. A child born to a Christian household, and whose mother is driven by faith and Christ would never allow her daughter to be indoctrinated into unhealthy rituals and traditions as she called it.

Every year as the festival comes around, elders in the community would meet up with the female priests whose jobs are to make preparations and needs of what to serve the goddess "Osun" herself, and how the day should go. After making a consultation with the Oracle, it's only by fate that a virgin girl would be picked to bear the sacrifice which will be presented on that day, but it does come with a lot of preparations and rituals which came as a shock and denial for the "Akinsanya" family.

"No way would I allow my daughter to do such a ridiculous and uncivilized thing!" Diane complained. She spoke out as soon as the message was delivered to her family. A child that came to her as a gift after waiting for ten years in marriage to have one, now the world wants to take her from them. More also her religion as a faithful Christian would never allow her to believe in such existence for tradition even if it is something that has been around way before they brought Christianity to their community.

"We should probably think about it, don't let us dissuade something that would cause trouble in the future!". Her husband warned. He is also a Christian, but believes that ways of their culture shouldn't be looked down upon just because they gave their lives to Christ. He would have them think twice before making a decision but his wife wouldn't want that.

"Are you suggesting we put our only daughter's life in danger so as to please the people? Are you even a good father? How can you not protect Destiny from such?" Diane ranted. She's only acting out as a mother that loves her daughter dearly, who else knows what would happen to destiny if she agrees to such?

"But I have seen many young maidens that were chosen in the past and are still living well till today. I can assure you that nothing bad will happen to our daughter!" Akin reassured his wife. He isn't one hundred percent agreeing to see his daughter go through the rituals that will take about two months before she carries the sacrifice, and not only will Destiny do so but will do so in confinement. No one would be able to see her or communicate with her for two months, as she's expected to be locked in a room where it's only her and the priestesses that will be preparing for the big day.

"So you're suggesting we sell her off to strangers? Making our daughter bears the sacrifice for everyone in the community? And you don't think that is against what we believe?" Diane couldn't make a sense of what her husband is yelping on, it would be better to inform their Church on the decision than to leave it to her husband alone to decide.

As decided, Daine took the matter up to the church. She was counseled to not be derailed from the path she has chosen to walk, and they all seem to disagree with the Oracle's choice. They think it's barbaric and audacious to select a sacrifice bearer who's not from their "occult group", not to mention that such a child belongs to God and not a non-living Goddess, to them the traditional way of communicating to God is unholy and unwelcomed. With their support, Daine could boldly give her reply to the priestesses, she's not ready to let go of her daughter to them.

"You can not change the will of the Gods, my daughter, you must accept fate and move on!". They warned her once again to think twice but the adamant Daine had made the decision for her daughter, and it was a no from her.

Just then, Destiny became sick, an illness that took a toll on her health. It all started after she had a nightmare of being chased by masquerades, when morning came she's already vomiting and couldn't eat. At first she was taken to the hospital for medical check-up, but all the test results came out to be negative as they couldn't find any particular illness to associate her with.

"I'm afraid nothing is wrong with your daughter!" The doctor confirmed. He has done his best to find the root of the problem but hasn't yet figured out one. It could be many things but none are visible enough to diagnose.

"If nothing is wrong with my daughter, then why is she still sick?". Daine complained. It's not like there is a paranormal activity going on in their household that could be the cause.

"I suggest you take her to a bigger hospital, she might get well from there!" The doctor made a suggestion of what seems like he is incapable of his work. They took his advice and seeked medical attention somewhere else bigger, unfortunately they also had something similar to say to them. With no help coming from anywhere, they took her home for nurture, but as time passed, her health couldn't improve.

The same priestesses visited again to remind them of the rituals that will begin sooner, but Diane kept repeating the same thing over again.

"I have told you numerous times that my daughter will not be a sacrificial lamb for anyone!".

"You should have thought the same before asking her from the Goddess Osun thirteen years ago? You were disturbed and troubled for not having a seed of the womb, you cried to Osun to hear your prayers and made a promise to never let the child depart from Osun, so why are you changing your mind now? Or is it because of your newfound faith?" One priestess reminded her of what she had forgotten many years back. As this came as a shock to her, it also was new to her husband who had no idea what his wife had done to have a child.

"You told me it was God's work, you never made any mention that our daughter was given to you by a goddess?" Akin felt betrayed by his wife's deceitfulness. The same woman that finds the Oracle repelling once begged for a child from Osun, yet she is still keeping such a child in danger.

"I had to do something or else your family would have you marry another woman and leave me. I was desperate to have one, a child that looks like you and I, but I had no other means than to go to Osun and begged for the fruit of the womb. Now see where that got me, the goddess wants my child back from me, I can't do that!". Daine confessed what she had kept in secret for many years but didn't sound convincing enough to please her husband. If his wife could take such a bold step yet act like she's not at fault, then she could do worse. A child born of his sperm and his wife's egg is made up of the spirit of a goddess, it's definitely a destiny they can't avoid.

"We have to let Destiny be the sacrifice bearer!". He proclaimed.

"What? That's not possible. We have to protect her, let's send her abroad!". She protested, not minding the present situation of their daughter.

"Abroad? Don't you want her to get well? We were told If she takes on the tasks she will get well. Aren't you a bad mother for preventing her from getting well?" He argued back.

"The church has warned me to not depart from the righteous paths and you shouldn't likewise!".

"The church? But you didn't get her from the church, did you?" Akin made a sarcastic remark to his wife who's being ridiculous in her thinking and saying. The two went back and forth at each other until Destiny spoke out herself for the first time, making a decision for herself.

"Mom, Dad, I will be the sacrifice bearer, so can you two stop arguing?". She has wanted to speak out on the matter ever since she saw the masquerades in her dream. She believes it's the universe sending her a warning and giving a second chance, so she has decided to do so.

"Honey, this is not for you to decide, you're still young so let's mommy decide for you!". Diane tried shutting her daughter down on the matter but Destiny wouldn't back out either.

"Mom, I'm doing this, it's my destiny!". She ran to her room upstairs after giving her decision but something in her felt strange, it was as if she never got sick at all when she walked the stairs to her room. That day she realized her sickness was definitely tied to her decision.

After a week of daily persuasion, Daine reluctantly agreed to let her daughter leave home for the two month ritual preparation. It was hard to say goodbye to her daughter, but it was all worth it in the end. The two months Destiny spent in the confined room, she learned a lot about tradition and ways of her people. She was taught many things by the priestesses, and it wasn't as bad as her mother had predicted it would be. While in confinement she didn't miss a single class of school work, a laptop was provided for her to receive lessons online while preparing for the big day ahead. She was taught the ritual dance which she will partake in on the very day, and also learned some chants in order to praise the Goddess. Even though she couldn't make contact with her parents physically, she could call them on phones whenever she was less busy, and it was great hearing back from her. The two months she spent in confinement had matured her reason and thinking, and would no longer berate the tradition of her own people because it's who they are as people. It was inspiring to hear the story about the goddess Osun, who is worshipped for her kindness, virtue, humility, and tranquility. She's the goddess of fertility and peace, and has chosen Destiny to be the sacrificial bearer. It's indeed an honor.

The day of the final event arrived, Destiny was dressed up in a traditional attire of cowries and white garment. She had on her head the big sacrificial bowl to which she carried some food stuffs such as fruits and even money. After months of heartfelt prayers, the sacrificial bowl was carried by her into the Osun temple which it was her alone to enter. Osun never welcomes anyone that's not pure, so it was Destiny that walked in with the bowl and came out with the message of prayers being answered. The celebration then began with people offering their gratitude to Osun or some people who stood by the river side to ask for favor from the Goddess, just as her own mother did thirteen years ago. People from far and wide came to celebrate with the community, as well as news reporters from all parts of the world who came to cover the story. When Destiny was asked to give an interview of what it feels like to be a virgin chosen to bear the sacrifice, she has more than one thing to say.

"Being born as a request from the Goddess made me think of myself as being special and also a living miracle for everyone that doesn't believe in our power as Africans. We are easily to abandon our culture for a newfound religion without questioning ourselves if God sure knows what he was doing when he made us Africans. I was chosen as a bridge between humanity and the heavens, and I can say I did my job right!".

Applauds followed after her impromptu speech for she was seen as a hero and the new face of spirituality that originates from us Africans.

CHAPTER TWENTY-EIGHT

BLUE DENDROBIUM

By Sohini Roy

4.30 AM.
Aarya leaned on the kitchen counter, her eyes looking somewhere in the direction of the lonely mynah sitting at her kitchen window. The tea has been over-steeped. It's bitter now. Not a great start to the day. Not a great day either.

The past couple of months have been so exhausting, it seems like she's aged more than she should have. And today, her face was the shade of winter fog. Her senses were sensing, but her brain was refusing to acknowledge them. Haze had wrapped her up in its translucent sorcery.

Aarya casually picked up her phone and opened the last chat. It was from her. The day has finally come.

When she had received the text, she'd read and re-read it a few times before replying. She couldn't wrap her head around the set of information and expectation that was being thrown at her that night. Her reply had also been too less for words weighing that heavy: a simple okay.

It cannot go on like this. Aarya threw the last quarter of the bitter tea into the dry sink next to her and left the empty cup on the counter, unwashed. Putting on her running shoes, a black hoodie, and a black mask, she went out for her morning stroll.

It was less of a stroll and more like she was desperately trying to run away from something, some grief, that her soul was silently mourning behind the hood and mask, even though her brain refused to accept it.

The vegetation around was as wet as Aarya's eyes, the dew on the grass dampening the end of her joggers near her ankle. When she could no longer keep the mask on, she tore it away from her face and sat by the little lake. She'd mindlessly run all through the park and reached the clearing, where the lake was, occasionally spotted by a few visitors. Everyone safely kept away from the chilly airs around the waterbody but it was nothing compared to the cold that radiated from inside Aarya. Unbothered, she sat, gasping for breath. Mind somewhere, soul somewhere, rationality somewhere, longings somewhere else.

Gone. He's... gone.

A small sob escaped her highly guarded individual. Her eyes resembled the surface of the lake, glassy and full, distorting her line of vision for a while before it trickled down her dry cheeks into a darkened trail on her hoodie, leaving her cheeks drier. She opened the file Dhriti had sent her and read it, carefully, holding the phone delicately, like it was a vintage paper that can tear apart anytime, along the folds, even from the minimum mishandling.

By the time Aarya was done absorbing the last letter into her being, the sun was already teasing the grey fog. The surface of the lake sparkled in places and vanished again.

The park was crowding up. Chaiwalas started frequenting more as the ones selling green coconuts and khajur ras started retreating. She got up, dusted her pants, and headed for the markets. It would be their last meeting. She has to be the winter sunshine, he used to call her, one last time.

9.37 AM.

Aarya parked her car at her old apartment and got off. The winter sun reflected off her white *kurti* and created a highly contrasting, cloudy white background for the bouquet of blue dendrobiums in her hands. They glistened with a turquoise and purple hue.

She was walking towards the main road, when Swati aunty, her old neighbor, noticed her.

"Aarya? *Arreh!* How are you? And all this white....um, everything okay *toh*?"

"Yeah. Actually, an old friend of mine died last night. I was going there. They'll be leaving soon, *Kaki*."

"*Ohho, na na,* you go. But sometimes come over and meet *Kaki* too...... It's been so long! Your parents are doing well, *toh* ?"

" Yes, *Kaki* ...and I will come. Don't worry. See you later." Aarya smiled at Swati aunty, a smile denied by the corners of her eyes. The winter wind cut through the chapped layers of her lips, as they cracked up even more with her efforts to fake a smile.

Everyone saw as Atlas lifted the weight of the blue skies on his bare shoulders. It was his punishment. Some rejoiced. The war was finally over and the bad have been punished. Some couldn't care any lesser. They got hypnotized by the patterns of white clouds flying through the clear, blue sky. Mesmerized they stared at the abode of their saviors. The handful that sympathized had no idea how heavy beautiful things can weigh. They measured in mortal scales, the immortal boundlessness of the eternal blue.

Aarya squared her shoulders as she crossed the roads. She was consciously fighting the invisible weight of an unknown sorrow on her broad shoulders.

The nearer she came, the heavier her breath became, until it was too much to hold at once, and a single, lonely tear trickled down her sunken cheeks, her eyes hollow, projecting a vision that lacked a fixed target. Then she had spotted the familiar white car that carries corpses: Swargarath.

The four corners of the car were adorned with tall tuberose sticks and bunches of burning incense. The sweet smell of the tuberose fought with the artificial aroma of the incense as Aarya approached the silence that surrounded the car in a circular array of humans of all ages. His worth was never restricted to any restrictions, be it age, gender, class, or creed. He's drawn happiness from all and imparted it as well. A little speck in that huge 'all' was Aarya herself.

Her lips started to quiver as she closed the distance and their corner started to sink and vibrate when her eyes fell on the old familiar face of sir, motionless; lost beyond material pain and agony, as his eyes pointed deadly at the corpse of his young son. Braj. There he lay, all mortal colors lost from his thin physique.

A sob escaped her tightly shut mouth as Aarya gazed at her first love. The love, that'd taught her she was loveable too, the love that'd included her, all those times she couldn't do it herself, the one who'd curled her face up in shy smiles for almost a decade, is gone. Too far beyond her reach. Too far beyond anybody's reach.

Aarya walked up to the file of people encircling Braj's corpse on the ground. A lady, maybe in her late forties, decorating his left-out body with sandalwood and tulasi leaves, her eyes raining occasionally on the white sheets that were hugging the pale corpse that once took up all the emptiness in Aarya's arms and her fragile heart.

Aarya silently looked around for a gap. She didn't want to be spotted by her unfortunate sports teacher. Baalu, Braj's cousin, was now standing next to Biju sir, holding the poor man who looked like he could collapse any moment and leave his poor fate behind, riding along with his only son. Baalu, himself, wasn't looking any better. All those scenes, of the two of them, running over, the cemented floors of the second storey of the old, sports club, teasing each other, adolescence dripping off their ripe frames, floated in the cold, December air. Aarya was once again standing at a distance experiencing the bubbly sounds of brotherhood. She has once again faded in the background. This time, Braj won't come to pull her out of it, include her into their games of joy and happiness, of friendship and young love.

She hadn't realized how long she'd stood there, crying subconsciously at the leftovers of her childhood friend, she got robbed last night. She missed her troublemaker smile. It filled up her eyes and overflowed, crawling down her blushing cheeks as newfound tears, with a warmth that could only be held by someone as passionate as Braj.

A cold hand pressed Aarya's biceps and she flinched immediately, turning towards the direction of its arm.

"Thank you for coming. At least now I know I could do something for him." Dhriti's eyes were swollen red from crying an entire night and probably more. She was Braj's girlfriend. If things had gone better, they would have gone over to fulfill their long-time relationship and Aarya would've never had to face her old wounds again. If only they had.

"Come this way," Dhriti crossed Aarya and was about to take her over to the remnants of her lost love when Aarya interrupted.

"Ah! Dhriti..." she spoke hesitantly, "Maybe you place it on him. I don't wish to be noticed by Sir. Or Baalu. Please."

"But he wanted you to," but Aarya shook her head, trying to persuade Dhriti. "Alright, come this way. From behind them. You can quietly place it from there and go... If you want to... I can't take that last wish away from him, Aarya... Please?"

Aarya looked down and silently followed Dhriti to a gap, halfway around the mass of mourners. She quietly extended her weakened limb forward and placed the bouquet on the hardened chest of his thin body. The blue of the dendrobiums shone like a jewel in the late morning sun. But, much to her disadvantage, she made direct eye contact with Baalu, while retreating. That was her cue. They burst into a hysterical fit of crying, eyes fixed on each other as their legs swam through the small yet difficult ocean of locals and reached near. And then they rained.

They rained, like the long-held showers of monsoon, they rained. They shared a sorrow that can't be experienced by a third one. Those days spent playing and giggling, together, among the dusty, webbed walls of the club, the team games and the racy singles matches, the small tricks invented at the board while the game was on, resulting in unexpected victories, the goofy fallouts over who shot it wrong. A pillar of their small castles have fallen down and the spilled stories lay homeless on the cold grounds. All they could do was hug tighter and cry, in hopes that the gap Braj had left behind could be met halfway at least.

Aarya carefully pulled away and held Baalu's arms, " Try and be strong. Someone else needs you more. Everyone of you," she pointed towards Biju Sir, Braj's father, with her eyes. " Today he's lost his entire home. When aunty died, at least Braj was there. He had faith in him. No one must've expected the events to take this sharp turn. Please be with him."

"I will." Baalu softly dropped Aarya's arms and scooted over to his devastated uncle. Aarya turned towards Dhriti and gave her a final hug before leaving.

"I know it feels different coming from your boyfriend's ex, but if you ever need help, feel free to contact me. Even if it means just talking."

"It was always different. You were always different. He's dated many, between you and me, but you were the one he was trying to find through them all, even through me. When his health degraded and he realized I was his last retreat, he got close to me, finally. All the stories about you, all the praises about you, that he carefully housed in himself, he shared with me. The way he talked about you, I knew I shall never be able to match you, but somewhere in between, we found our safe space. You were like the star in the night sky he liked to gaze at. Even when we sat, holding each other. He always said you'll be replaceable. Perhaps, leaving you was the only regret he ever had. That's why, when his health sensed his time was nearing its end, he told me to give you the letter. He'd once written it after he broke up with you. He added something to it, on his deathbed and handed me. And I rushed to find you. What more could I do? I loved him hopelessly."

"He was someone who deserved that kind of hopeless love, an undying passion, and care, no matter where he wandered. You were the last gift the fates had offered him.

He was lucky, indeed, to have someone like you." They smiled lightly at each other. It wasn't fake, but it took so much effort that its impact got lessened.

Dhriti turned towards the *swargarath* as Braj's corpse was being mounted into the car. She faded among the mourners, while Aarya turned around and walked away. As far as she could, with her childhood memories safe with her being, carefully tied by an unexpected last letter from a past lover and friend.

Love is a ritual. Its absoluteness lies in its casual solemnity. It is a precious flower that likes to bloom on the tree of patience in the jungle of time. Its beauty confuses cautious eyes. As if the spirits tend to it there. It dances to its own tune, it imparts fragrance without asking for someone to smell it. Some float in its aroma, some swim hypnotized, but those that drown, find the honey dripping at the base of its stalk underneath its artistry.

Aarya's vision cleared as she crossed the road and headed back to her old apartment where she'd parked her grey WagonR. She left her old neighborhood and headed back home. The new one where she now resided.

Epilogue

August 13, 2013,

Every smile I see, reminds me of your shy, plump cheeks. Every game I play, seem bland. I miss your little tricks. I revisit the club once in a while and the stairs leading to the closed, green doors, get me excited. Like I'd pull them open to see you playing again. We were perfect. Just as we were. Every face I see, I miss yours. I spot you on the streets once in a while when you cross the roads with your father. I silently watch. If nothing else, I long to watch you like that, everyday.

    I know I broke up abruptly. I was a fool. I have had my share of punishment. I have rejected the more and settled. And now, like that wasn't enough already, I am being greedy, once again. We both deserved a proper closure to the relationship. We didn't get to have one. And my time is far lesser than yours. I won't be able to give it to you, but as my last wish, if you can, then bring me a bunch of your favourite blue dendrobiums. The ones we used to buy, from your favourite florist's. I'll think I had finally met you before I leave. I know you would try to avoid it as much as possible but think of it as a request from your friend Braj, rather than your ex. And if you can, somehow, try and find your share of the closure too. You know how incapable I've always been. See how I'm going to die with all my regrets attached! Soon you'll be reading this, but not too soon. I have asked Dhriti to give it to you, but haven't told her where to look for you. She knows you're not on social platforms. As much I want this to reach you, I don't want to burden you with my selfish interests. If you can convince yourself without pressing too hard, then do come to bid me the farewell.

Your "friend",
Braj.

Books By Writefluence

WriteFluence is an innovative literary arts consultancy featuring worthy authors and showcasing their talent. WriteFluence provides literary services such as publishing, book editing, proofreading, book designing, author branding, and book promotions.

Until September 2022, we have worked with over 500 writers from all over the world. 19 of our international compilations are now available for purchase on Amazon with worldwide distribution to over 170 countries.

We hold regular creative writing contests, and your submissions go through a rigorous screening process by not just our editorial team; we invite jury members to judge your work for a fair selection process.

Books curated by WriteFluence:

- Wafting Earthy is a compilation of the winning short stories of the international premier league short-story contest PenFuenza, organized by WriteFluence. The book consists of 31 literary pieces in different genres, based on the theme of 'Fragrances'. The stories were selected from a whopping 142 submissions that had been received from all over the world for the contest. PenFluenza, described as one of the most comprehensive creative writing contests by several online entities was indeed structured that way to make sure the best of writers could be brought together under one book cover. The contest had a theme, a specific word limit, and a very proficient jury.

- In January 2021, WriteFluence announced their very first exclusively-for-women-writers story-writing contest FemmeFluenza and received 79 entries in a span of just a month! Out of my BOX is a collection of the winning stories written by the selected women writers, alongside the theme of celebrating womanhood and surviving through various challenges it brings along.
- Spent is a curated collection of winning poems from amongst 200+ submissions received on this poetry writing prompt based on the theme of Erotica; contest held by WriteFluence from December 2020 - January 2021.
- Dear Ma, is a compilation of beautiful letters written by 19 writers to their mothers to celebrate the occasion of International Mother's Day, 2021!
- Tickled Pink is a compilation of winning poetry written by the winners of High5 - The great poetry hunt contest organized by WriteFluence, celebrating the occasion of 5 months of successful WriteFluencing!
- The Other Side is a compilation of the winning short stories of the international short-story contest organized by WriteFluence in April-May 2021 and based on the genre of horror/supernatural/suspense/sci-fi/thriller (fiction). The book consists of 36 short stories written by 33 prolific writers, that were selected from 301 submissions that had been received from all over the world for the contest. The book also features 13 winning poems selected from the promotional contest 'The Other Side' that was run for the book, prior to its release.
- Locked Up is a compilation of the winning stories/essays/poems written by children for the PenFluenza Junior writing contest organized by WriteFluence in

2021 about their feelings around the pandemic and everything about the covid lock-down.
- The Land of Infinite Summer is a compilation of the winning short stories written by writers all over the world for the WriteFluenza contest organized by WriteFluence in June-July 2021. The book consists of 20 short stories written by 19 prolific writers, and were selected from 209 submissions that had been received from all over the world for the contest.
- Purrfect Surprise is a compilation of the winning stories from the WriteFluenza contest organized by WriteFluence in June 2021. The book consists of short stories selected from 209 submissions that had been received from all over the world for the contest.
- Mrs. Rosewood is a compilation of the winning stories from the Mrs. Rosewood contest organized by WriteFluence in June 2021. The book consists of short stories selected from 82 submissions that had been received from all over the world for the contest.
- Standstill is a collection of winning sonnets written by winners of the Sonnetto and Augustanza contest, 2021, and were selected out of a total of 184 submissions received for both the contests.
- Rubble House is a compilation of the winning stories from the WriteFluenza contest organized by WriteFluence in June 2021. The book consists of short stories selected from a whopping 209 submissions that had been received from all over the world for the contest.
- A Lie On Her Lips is a compilation of the winning stories from the LGBTQ Romance / Betrayal short story contest organized by WriteFluence in July-August 2021. The book consists of short stories selected from 173

submissions that had been received from all over the world for the contest and the stories are based on the theme of betrayal.
- Spookoween is a compilation of 20 spooky winning short stories selected from a collection of 97 submissions received from all over the world for the Spookoween contest organized by WriteFluence in September-October 2021. Here's a spine-chilling book full of stories that won't let you sleep.
- Hashtag, Not a Phase is a compilation of the winning stories from the LGBTQ Romance / Betrayal short story contest organized by WriteFluence in July-August 2021. The book consists of short stories selected from 173 submissions that had been received from all over the world for the contest and the stories are based on the theme of LGBTQ Romance.
- Cloud 9 is a compilation of the winning stories from the Children's Day special short story contest by the same name organized by WriteFluence in October 2021. The book consists of 16 short stories selected from 107 submissions that had been received from all over the world for the contest.
- SEPIA is a compilation of the winning short stories of the international premier league short-story contest PenFuenza 2.0, organized by WriteFluence. The book consists of 32 literary pieces written in different genres and based on the theme of A Photograph, and were selected from a whopping 153 submissions that had been received from all over the world for the contest.
- Out of my BOX 2 is a compilation of the winning short stories written by women writers, during the short-story contest FemmeFuenza 2.0, organized by WriteFluence. The book consists of 19 literary pieces

written in different genres alongside the theme of celebrating womanhood and surviving through various challenges it brings along and were selected from 108 submissions that had been received from all over the world for the contest.
- Mr. Rosewood is a compilation of the winning short stories written by women writers, during the short-story contest organized by WriteFluence. The book consists of short stories selected from 58 submissions that had been received from all over the world for the contest.
- The Other Side II is a compilation of the winning short stories written by women writers in the Genre: Horror / Supernatural / Suspense / Sci-Fi / Thriller (fiction) based on the prompt or theme 'The Other Side'. The book consists of 14 literary pieces that were selected from 49 submissions that had been received from all over the world for the contest.
- Crimson is a collection of the winning short stories written by writers across the globe for The Open Theme Contest organized by WriteFluence. The book consists of 21 literary pieces that were selected from 97 submissions that had been received from all over the world for the contest.

Milton Keynes UK
Ingram Content Group UK Ltd.
UKHW010629150923
428743UK00001B/28